THE TRUE STORY OF
an Alaska Native and her fight to end abuse

HIS HAND UPON ME

Katherine Gottlieb

MBA, DPS, LHD

DAUGHTER OF MARGARET SHUGAK AND ALFRED QUIJANCE

RETELLING, LLC

ISBN-13: 978-1-7350013-9-5

Published by Retelling | retelling.net
Cover design by Cynthia Young | youngdesign.biz

This book is dedicated to my husband Kevin Gottlieb;

our children Angelique, Tanya, Marie, Monica, Timothy, and Esther;

their spouses and my grandchildren and great-grandchildren.

INTRODUCTION

WHEN I THINK BACK on my life, I wonder why some memories remain crystal clear, as if they happened last week, and others are hazy, as if I'm watching them through a thick fog that occasionally lifts, revealing some little piece of my past, if clear only for a moment. Some of my childhood is not completely clear to me. It's like I don't know the whole story to parts of my own life.

I didn't have an easy childhood. My siblings and I lived in a war zone of alcoholism, domestic violence, abuse and neglect. I have many clear—even happy—memories from my early childhood. Then life became chaotic in our home. My memories of the abuse and neglect that followed appear more like snapshots, fragments of experiences that terrified me as a child.

Yet, I wonder how it can be that my siblings who may have witnessed or experienced the same events as I, remember them differently, or remember parts of a particular story that I don't. I do not doubt the things I remember actually happened, but there are many gaps in my memory. And there are still questions in my mind about what is the real truth about my family. Secrets and confusion followed the chaos that overtook our lives.

For example, several years ago I was at a large event when a woman I'd never met approached me.

She said, "You have a sister living that you have not met. You need to get ahold of her so you all can be reunited." Then she disappeared into the crowd and I never heard from her again.

Do I have a lost sister? If I do, I hope we can find one another. Maybe we can help each other answer some of the questions from my patchy memory.

When I first began to reflect on my past, I pictured myself fully grown. It wasn't until much later I realized I had actually once been a child. It happened while watching a video of a young six-year-old lying on a rug, drawing a picture, while speaking to a counselor. She had long black hair and brown skin. She could have been me.

As I listened to her speak about herself, it shocked me when I realized, I was also so innocent and little, once, a long time ago.

CHAPTER 1

My father emigrated from the Philippines at the age of 17. He told stories of what it was like to grow up in the provinces and how he ran away from home to live in Manila. There he learned to steal and pick pockets to help feed the other homeless children he lived with in the city. At the age of 17 he got on a ship and came to America.

He was small in stature, only 4'11", but my father worked hard and soon earned his citizenship. He also quickly got into gambling. In time, he became the head of a big gambling network in California and owned three houses. He assisted many of his friends with housing and food when they were in need and helped many Filipinos become citizens of the United States. But eventually all the gambling activities disappeared from his life, along with the money and houses, as happens with so many people with a gambling lifestyle, and he began the life of a cook.

He traveled to Alaska to cook for the Filipino men working in the cannery in a small Kodiak village called Shearwater. That was where he met my mother. Mom was also 4'11", a small, beautiful *Sugpiaq* woman with pale skin and pitch-black hair. She had been born in Old Harbor, a small village a few miles away, and had two brothers and a sister. When my parents married, my mother was only 16 years old.

They moved to California, where my three older siblings were born. Then Mother became homesick so they returned to Alaska so they could live closer to her family in Old Harbor. I was born during the time we lived back in Alaska. My mom named me after her sister Katherine who died young of pneumonia.

Sometime during the first two years of my life, Dad got a job at a restaurant in Seattle so we moved again, leaving my oldest brother with Gramma to raise.

Dad worked as a cook at a Wharf restaurant in Seattle. In addition to his Filipino dishes, he learned how to cook Chinese food. We grew up learning how to cook the best Asian food. We ate Filipino delicacies like *lumpia* and *adobo chicken.* (Years later, it was not uncommon for some of my siblings and me to be sent to stay at other people's homes for periods of time. We never knew why or when it would happen. We would stay with friends, relatives, or in foster homes. I once stayed with a couple who were Filipino and white. I have no idea why I was there. To me, their home seemed the size of a mansion. I was delighted to see rice being served for breakfast, but they put milk and raisins in it! This would never do for a child raised on Filipino food. I wouldn't eat it.)

We lived in a two-story house, in the Beacon Hill section of Seattle, a safe neighborhood with nice sidewalks. My crib was in the warm carpeted bedroom where Mom and Dad slept.

As a small child, I saw my father as kind and gentle. I was a Daddy's girl with an undying love for him. Whenever I felt sick, I climbed onto the bed with him. He would rub my tummy and hold me until I fell asleep. I always felt safe with him.

When Mom would tell Dad he had to spank us, he would take off his belt and we would all run upstairs and climb under blankets. Coming into the room, he would holler, "Don't do that again!" Lifting his belt high in the air, only to let it fall lightly on our blankets, we would pretend to be hurt and yell, "Ouch, ouch, okay, okay!" while we muffled our giggles.

Sometimes when Dad came home in the afternoons, I would reach for him as he walked in the door. Putting his finger to his lips he'd disappear around the corner. Soon he would bring me milk in a bottle, and I'd run upstairs to drink it. Mom would have been furious if she had known what he was doing.

Our mother established the rule that we had to sit at the dinner table until we had eaten all of our food. Some of us fell asleep, face first into our plates, unable or not wanting to finish our food. I hated vegetables of any kind. When Mom wasn't looking, Dad would grab my vegetables and stuff them in his mouth. I tried hard not to grin and give our secret away.

My father loved me. He had only good words for me and made me feel special, unique, intelligent, and strong. I don't believe I would have known love from a human without his love for me as a young child.

I did not feel this love from my mother. I only remember my mother holding me one time. I don't know why, but she let me come sit beside her on the couch and she put her arm around me, pulling me to her side. I was tucked into her body. I can still feel it today. When my little brother Kenty was born four years after me, we all went to the hospital to see him. I climbed up on a short little box to kiss him on the forehead while Mom held him. He was so beautiful, with lots of dark black hair. As Mom lay in the bed holding him, I watched them, wishing I could crawl up in the bed and be held by her too.

When I was around the age of four or five, our family moved to a section of Seattle known as Georgetown. It was to become the place of both my happiest childhood memories and the birthplace of my personal nightmares.

The tiny town rested against a tree-covered hill. The county building with a big clock at its peak sat in the middle of town next to a small hotel. Sidewalks lined the cobbled streets in front of a local grocery store, a bar, a small-town drug store, and an ice cream shop where we could buy a cone with one giant scoop for a nickel.

A short unpaved street ran in front of our home. Old houses filled with families lined both sides. The next street was paved and filled with middle-class homes. I walked each day to the compact elementary school five blocks away from our home.

Our older, two-story house had discolored tiled floors, painted walls, an old wooden front porch and a detached garage. A clothes line stood in the backyard for hanging out the wash. The two large windows in the living room in the front of the house overlooked the barren front yard. Mom and Dad always promised to plant grass in the dirt-covered front yard, but it was always just dirt, sometimes dusty, sometimes muddy. A broken, patched-together fence of mixed wire and wood enclosed the yard. I didn't mind, it was good for playing in.

An old electric stove fueled the tiny kitchen, with a small table pushed against steps that led upstairs. If we touched the counter and the stove just right we would get a gentle shock. A big pile of laundry always waited to be done in the small enclosed back porch that had been converted into a laundry room. The dining room had a wood floor we would slide across in our stocking feet after it had been waxed. Just off the dining room, our one bathroom held a giant old-fashioned clawfoot bathtub. My little sister and I would soap up the entire tub to slide up and down it. Upstairs were two bedrooms and a small hallway.

How we all fit in this house, I cannot account. I had three older siblings and several younger siblings. In the following years, more children were born back-to-back. Mother had 14 children, including two miscarriages.

My siblings and I always shared beds, never sleeping alone. Mom and Dad had the big room, with an extra large closet where all our clothes were kept. They converted the dining room into another place to sleep—with one couch, one bed, and a crib.

Along the unpaved road in our neighborhood, a few tall old trees grew in the yards, one with small green apples. One time my siblings and I picked a couple of the apples from our neighbor's yard. He dragged us by our arms to our mother, and in an angry voice yelled, "They are stealing our apples!" We were just hungry.

I loved when my older siblings took us out on adventures. Sometimes we walked several miles, under the overpass, into the depths of the city. We would scrounge up enough change to ride the bus back home.

My older sister, Sarah, was an important part of my childhood. She would often come up with elaborate pretend games to play, assigning the rest of us our roles. Pretend lives, pretend reality, make-believe princesses and queens, pretending to have lots of pretty things and plenty of food to eat.

— Reflection —

*I loved to pretend. My imagination was free to go any-
where it wanted to. It was very real to me, though I always
knew I was pretending. I could pretend to fly, pretend to be
a great trapeze artist, pretend everything was wonderful in
my world. I made up a nameless, invisible friend who would
follow me when we drove places with our family. This friend
could kind of fly, but mostly ran very fast. As we drove I
would, in my mind, help it jump over big rocks or swerve so
as not to hit trees.*

*I understand now that using my imagination was a form
of protection for me in my childhood. It gave me an escape
and rest from the chaos and pain of our home. I could use my
imagination to shut out the real world, replacing it with the
imaginary one, with me as the primary actor.*

*Later in my life God placed His finger on this issue as an
area in which to change. I learned instead, to tear down the
wall, invite Him in and then to use the creative imagination
He has gifted me with for good.*

Beautiful, smart, tough and strong, Sarah was our protector.
When she knew kids were picking on us, she would go after them
and suddenly they would leave us alone. On occasion during the
evenings when our parents were not home, I would follow Sarah out
onto the roof and sit looking up at the stars. She would sometimes
sneak out of the house at night and let me go with her to meet up
with her friends. When we would come home, Dad would scream at

her and yell, "Why were you out? What were you doing?" But Sarah was very protective of me and would often send me back home, not letting me stay out with her.

As children, we often played in the large, vacant lot next to our house. We kicked through the grass until the grasshoppers jumped. We would capture them and they would spit in our hands; it looked like they were chewing tobacco. Sometimes we would sneak into the hotel in town, creep up the stairs and run through the hallways, escaping down the other side through the side exit. We also played in and near the big garage by the side of the house. Once, a neighbor boy named Tommy and I pretended we were getting married. Our playmates dressed us up, putting a white dress on me with a long blue train, which was actually a tarp that came from a stack of old tires down the street.

One of my favorite places to play was on a nearby street where a lumber company stored large old beams. I would climb up on them and run and jump beam to beam pretending that I was avoiding crocodiles below me. Had I fallen, they were high enough off the ground that I could have easily been hurt.

The railroad yard was down at the bottom of the hill. I loved going down there and climbing into and all over the cars. Down the street a tire company stored hundreds of old tires in huge piles and stacks. We would climb to the very top and jump from one stack to another playing tag.

We lived not far from the railroad tracks, and Boeing airplanes often flew over our home. "Poop Bombers! Poop Bombers!" my younger sister, Lulu and I would scream as we ran for cover. In our innocent minds, we always thought if they flushed the toilets on the planes, it would come pouring down on our heads.

Lulu was one year younger than me. Her real name is Axenia, but I nicknamed her Lulu because I couldn't say her name when I was little, and the name stuck. Mom favored Lulu. I knew it, but it never bothered me. I was glad she was loved. Lulu and I did everything together and were especially close.

Our hair was down to our waists. I hated when Mom would decide to brush and fix our long hair. She would hit us if we winced or cried out because it hurt so much. Lulu and I would laugh at each other when she was done and say, "China man! China man!" because our hair was pulled back so tight it made our eyes turn up.

One of our jobs was to do the laundry with the old washing machine on the back porch. We'd make suds and lather up our faces to play Santa Clause. Once, Lulu accidently swallowed a mouthful of soap suds. We both were scared and quit playing the game. Our hair or our hands often got caught in the wringer as we stuck clothes through it. One of us would hit the emergency handle to make it stop and pop open. We hung the clothes on the lines out in the backyard to dry.

Both Lulu and I had our tonsils taken out at the same time. I was told it was because I was too skinny and the doctors didn't like it, so I needed my tonsils out. We were placed together in the same room in Swedish Hospital, where we played with the nurse call button, driving the hospital staff crazy. Lulu and I asked each other if we would rather jump out the window or get our tonsils out. We both agreed we would rather jump out the window.

CHAPTER 2

"IT'S FOR YOU!" I said to Mom.

I held up the art project I had made in kindergarten at school, covered in pretty paper flowers. I stood outside on the porch, excited to surprise her as she opened the door to greet me.

"Ooh! It is so beautiful," Mom said as she smiled and took it, gently placing it on the wall.

In those early years, Mom had a wonderful laugh and her smile brightened the room. And she threw the best birthday parties.

"Happy Birthday to you! Happy Birthday to you!" Mom's nightingale voice would ring out as she carried the cake lit with candles. Giggling children with smiling faces would line the stairs, laughing and playing in every room.

Mom never worked outside of the home. She filled the house with her music, playing the guitar and accordion, often singing along in her beautiful voice.

"Que sera, sera, whatever will be will be, the future's not ours to see, so que sera sera, what will be, will be."

She would sing to the babies, "Ah—lodido dido…dido dido.. ah—lodido..dido," while she taught them to wave their little hands side to side and dance to her singing.

On our outings, we would play games in the car. Going through a tunnel, we would all begin singing together as fast as we could,

"You are my sunshine, my only sunshine,

you make me happy when skies are grey,

you'll never know dear,

how much I love you,

please don't take my sunshine away!"

The game was to finish the song before the end of the tunnel. Mom's beautiful voice led us and we always finished with giggles and laughter.

In late summer our family went to pick beans at a local farm. My sister Lulu and I raced each other to see who could gather the most. Each basket earned us 25 cents. At the end of the day, our parents combined the money we all earned and took us for fast food. I always ordered French fries and ice cream, while the others ordered French fries and hamburgers. Then we would head to the drive-in movies. Mom and Dad let us stay on the swings or sit on top of the car to watch. As nighttime darkened and crickets chirped, we little ones usually fell asleep before the movie ended, unless it was a scary one.

Once we were all at Pike's street market, shopping with our parents. I was about nine at the time. A young girl was at the market with her parents, and Mother pulled us aside to introduce her. "Meet Janet; she is your sister," said Mother, who had adopted her out to a Filipino couple who had been raising her. We hadn't known she existed until that day. I gave her the nickname "Ya Ya Jean" because I couldn't pronounce the name Janet. We all instantly accepted her; she was the sixth oldest sibling in our family. Through the years after she remained in constant connection with our family, once traveling to Alaska to meet her relatives.

One day I found a dog in the schoolyard and she followed me home. We found the owners of the dog, who said I could have her, and by some miracle my mother let me keep her. Her name was Susie.

I discovered I could teach Susie to do tricks. I taught her to jump over the fence and pull me on a sled. Before long, she got pregnant and I witnessed her giving birth to her puppies in the laundry room. She was very protective of her babies and wouldn't let anyone touch or go near them, except me. I loved her deeply and as only a dog can do, she loved me in return. Susie was more than just a dog to me during those years in Georgetown.

Those were the happy days.

I am thankful for the good memories, full of fun times and happiness, the times we seemed like a regular family. The birthdays, Mom singing, playing the guitar and accordion, cooking dinners, regular outings to movies, long drives, and visiting other relatives. There were a lot of us crammed into a small space with lots of noise and chaos. We were poor, but didn't know it. Our lives were going to take a dramatic course of change, but we didn't know that either.

CHAPTER 3

I always had the feeling someone was watching over me. It gave me the confidence to try daring things other children my age wouldn't. I would swing the highest on the school swings, and flip around the monkey bars, high above the ground like a trapeze artist. I would walk for miles around the neighborhood. I found hills and cliffs to climb. I was fearless. I was never afraid to be alone; I liked it.

From as far back as I can remember, God has been a part of my life. My father was Catholic and my mom was Russian Orthodox. Icons of Mary and Jesus hung on the walls of our home. In one corner, an icon with a candle burned most of the time, representing the Russian Orthodox church.

I spoke to God often from a very early age. I would kneel in front of Mother Mary and Jesus, looking into their eyes, and I would pray and pray. I knew God could hear me and see me through these images of Mary and Jesus.

A Christian missionary from my mother's hometown of Old Harbor, Alaska, would drop by and visit once in a while. I loved her visits. Her bright face and soft voice had a calming influence in our home during her times with us. She looked like an angel.

We went to both Catholic and Russian Orthodox churches.

Occasionally we found ourselves in a charismatic Protestant church.

One Sunday the Protestant pastor said, "If you believe what Jesus has done on the cross to pay for your sins, and want to ask Him to be your Savior, you can pray this prayer with me." I bowed my head to pray. "Jesus, we believe you came to die on the cross for our sins, and we ask you to forgive us and to come live inside us." I knew I wanted to go to heaven. I knew I wanted to be washed of all my sins, and I believed Jesus died for me.

I was so excited, I could hardly wait to go home and tell my parents. When I told my mom, she responded, "Don't ever speak about this again." I thought she would be happy for me. Mother never explained herself when she made statements like this.

Although she told me not to speak about my experience, she didn't stop me from attending church in the little white chapel. I learned the stories of David and Goliath, Jonah and the whale, and Noah and the ark. I loved all the Sunday school songs, like *Jesus Loves Me* and *Jesus Loves the Little Children*. I went to as many summer activities as I could, where I would hear Bible stories and learn all the church camp songs. I especially loved the breaks when they served cookies and milk.

I don't remember much about the Catholic church, but I clearly remember the Russian Orthodox church, and I'm still flooded with awe whenever I enter one. As a child, the ornate beauty of the church, the smell of incense, the large pictures of angelic powerful men and angels, made it seem as though God would appear at any moment. We were all expected to be extremely quiet: no talking, no giggling, no wiggling as we stood through the entire service. We didn't know what the priests were saying. They were magnificent, too, dressed in robes with their great big hats and long beards. I loved the taste of the wine and the little bit of bread served to us at communion. At the time, I didn't understand what it all meant but I knew it was a very sacred part of worshipping God.

CHAPTER 4

THEN LIFE SEEMED TO change overnight. Mom began to drink.

Something happened in Mom's life to cause her overuse of alcohol. We never learned why. Perhaps she couldn't handle having so many children so close together to take care of. I don't know. All I know is our family experienced an abrupt change. The innocence of my childhood ended quickly as our lives began to revolve around her drinking.

There were times when, as she began to drink in the evening, she would be jovial and fun. She'd clear the dining room—with the waxed floor, perfect for dancing—and put music on the record player. Then she would teach us how to dance. We learned the jitterbug and the waltz. We would partner up and dance far into the night. Mom laughed, danced, and played with the babies.

Soon she began drinking early in the morning until she passed out. Only beer at first, then Thunderbird in the evenings. She often passed out on the floor or wherever she happened to be.

I missed her singing. Instead of hearing her beautiful voice singing the popular songs of the day, now she screamed and cursed, her voice thick and her words slurred. Added to the normal chaos and noise of a large family were the sounds of breaking glass, bodies slamming into walls, violence in the night, the smell of stale beer and vomit, and the unforgettable sound of flesh hitting flesh.

— Reflection —

I recently was on a flight where a man hit another man. It immediately sent terror in my heart—that sound—the sound of flesh hitting flesh with the violent voice, the growling anger of the man swinging his fist, hitting the other man. I remembered what it was like to witness this as a little child. I had seen the adults as giants in height, pushing and shoving each other, fist hitting the flesh of the other, causing blood to splatter over me in the air and then on me. Sheer horror and helplessness, but raising an inner strength inside of me to protect—protect my little siblings, the babies, my mother.... I was five years old.

"Mom, Mom," one of us would reach out carefully and take the cigarette from her hand. "Mom, you're scaring us." She would be smoking and would go into some type of stupor. Her eyes would glaze over and she couldn't see us, even though we were standing right in front of her. It scared all of us children when this happened.

I was in kindergarten and would often be the first to get home from school. The smell of beer, alcohol, and dirty diapers would hit me as I entered the house. Many times, I found Mother passed out and the babies crying. I would run around comforting them. I picked up beer cans and bottles and threw them away, then cleaned up around the house and changed the dirty diapers.

Sometimes, I would find my mother on the floor, naked. I already knew I couldn't pick her up, nor could I wake her because I had tried many times. I would cover her naked body as she lay passed out. If we had canned milk, I would fix some milk in bottles and feed the babies. If not, I would gently lay a baby next to Mom, pulling her breast out so the baby could feed while Mother slept. I didn't know the alcohol in her system could be passed on to my siblings through her milk. I was only five and I had never heard of such a thing. I was always afraid she would turn over and squash the baby, or worse yet, wake up swinging her fists in anger.

There were times when I found myself standing in front of a bar, trying to get her to come home to feed the baby because I knew she had breast milk and we didn't have any milk in the house. Our mother's drinking started abruptly and progressed quickly.

— Reflection —

Pictures of us when we were little reflect in our eyes all the harm that happened. Childhood innocence is gone. When we as children are being harmed, our walk isn't as light and there is no skipping as we run. Our stringy hair hangs in our faces over our eyes, to cover our shame. Our laughter has no joy; it's more hushed and our play is quiet with quick glances over our shoulders. Our eyes look down, more than up, when we were engaging in conversation. And we wince or step back when someone near raises their hand to fix their hat or move toward us to try to brush the hair from our faces. We seem older, wiser, too wise for a young child.

Where has all my innocence gone?
At five years old
 I looked in the mirror
And I beheld innocence and beauty.
My play was frivolous and carefree
My laughter was filled with screams of glee.

There was no fear in my heart
I trusted all people.
I walked in dark places without fear
There was sunshine in my soul.

I had normal desires.
I longed for someone to love me.
I wanted to be cherished,
To be adored.

Where has all my innocence gone?

Today, I often think about the loss of a child's innocence as I watch our grandchildren. They run screaming with joy through the house, giggling, carefree. When the music plays, they dance with freedom, twirling around and around. When it's bath time, they strip down without any shame—jumping in the tub, sometimes two at a time. Children without fear, standing defiantly with a voice, stating, "I don't want to eat my vegetables!" Or, "I don't want to go to bed!" What an awesome thing to behold, children without fear, not ashamed and having a voice.

CHAPTER 5

As the size of our family continued to grow, so did my mother's dependence on alcohol. And so did the physical abuse, which was especially bad when she ran out of something to drink or was sobering up. She would often tie us up in chairs and sit us in front of the TV. She began pulling our hair, often walking away with clumps of hair in her fists. She would pinch us until we bruised, slap us until our mouths bled, whip us with belts, and scream horrible things at us. Her favorite weapon of choice was her fists. Hitting us on our heads with her knuckles was common.

I stood on my little stool doing the dishes one day, when Mom came into the kitchen. Finding some spot I had missed, she rapped my head hard with her knuckles. Knowing more was coming, I made the mistake of ducking the next blow. That only made her angrier and the following blows worse.

One time while doing the dishes, I put a pot on my head knowing she would be coming after me and thinking the pot would protect me. Sure enough, she did, and slammed her knuckles into the pot. My ears rang all day long. I didn't do that again.

My siblings and I soon learned the rules of enduring her abuse. We learned not to duck or even twitch a muscle as she passed by. If we ever avoided a blow, the following hits would be twice as hard or twice as many. We learned never to cry, even when one of the other kids were being beaten. To cry meant giving her the opportunity to "give us something to cry about." I actually learned to cry out of one eye, the eye that wasn't facing her.

When she would call for us, it was best to have little or no expression on our faces. Don't look guilty. Don't look scared. Never look happy, look completely blank. We lived in absolute terror of her. She could freeze us in our tracks with just a look or a snap of her fingers.

We all understood that to have our name called by Mom while she was drinking meant we had better get in her presence as fast as possible. We knew if we didn't, it would be worse later when she caught us. We believed we had nowhere else to go. This was our home. And this had become our life.

CHAPTER 6

Mom began to bring men home with her from the bars. Dad also invited his friends to come visit. One of the men would hang around the house, making himself known as a friend. He began to abuse me. He would catch me alone in the downstairs bathroom or upstairs in our bedroom. It seemed like he knew when no one else would be around.

I didn't understand what he was doing. I felt like he was crushing me on the bed. He was very large and I was tiny. I finally decided to tell my mother. She was sitting on the couch, and I was standing in front of her. I tried to tell her that he was hurting me and describe what he was doing.

Mom stopped me and slapped me across the face.

"You wicked little girl! Never speak to me about this again and don't tell anyone!"

In that moment, and in ways I couldn't yet begin to understand, my mother defined me.

"You wicked little girl."

For years and years to come, I believed that to be the truth about me. It explained every bad thing that happened to me from that point on. It was the reason why she didn't hold me, or say she loved me. I never heard those words from her. It was why I was unlovable, unwanted, and used. I longed for that hug, longed to feel adorable and cherished. It was the reason I did unexplainable and harmful things to myself and others. It was the reason my life was the way it was.

You wicked little girl!

I drowned in shame. I had been ruined somehow, and I was silenced. I believed this evil thing that was happening was somehow caused by my own wickedness. There was no one I could talk to about it. My heart was broken and I didn't understand.

From then on, I dreaded going to my mother when she called me. I felt ashamed. It covered me, and I felt it. My innocence was gone, I was worthless, ugly and dirty. Something had changed. It seemed like Mom knew, too, because when she would call me and I approached her, cowering, she would tell me what she had to say, then kick me to send me on my way.

If Mom would have responded, "Oh, my sweet baby girl. Let me hold you. This man did a very bad thing to you and I will never let him harm you again. Don't be afraid, you didn't do anything wrong. It is good that you told me. I will do something about it," my entire reflection on life would have changed.

I began locking the door when I took a bath. I didn't want anyone to come in when I was there. I loved the solitude and feeling of safety. Many times, I would take my baby brothers with me and they would fall sound asleep in the haven of the warm water that covered us. I love warm baths today.

No one knew what was happening to me. My abuse was mine to bear and I found ways to live with it.

I do not believe my mother ever knew the impact of her words. I don't believe she knew what to do when I told her. I don't know what she had been taught. I don't know what her early childhood experiences were like.

That man who smothered and crushed my body, who touched me in inappropriate ways, who made me do things that I should never have experienced, stole my innocence as a child. He made me feel dirty and unclean. What he did planted shame deep in my heart. It changed what I believed about myself and how I experienced life. He caused me to experience things that were not meant for my body to know or mind to understand at that age. I would never know what purity would feel like as a teenager, let alone innocence. He stole from me the experience I could have had of God's beautiful design in the act of becoming one with your spouse.

I Knew

I knew I was wicked
I knew I was ugly
I knew something was wrong with me
I knew I was not pure
I knew I was not good
I knew I was not like everyone else
I knew I was unlovable
I knew whenever something bad happened to me
*   that I deserved it somehow*
I knew I had no choices
I knew I couldn't escape
I knew I was alone.

This was the first of many abuse experiences that came later from different men. Often, when men abused me I would freeze. I couldn't move, nor run, nor protest. I didn't know how. I felt it was wrong, but I couldn't tell anyone, so life just went on.

CHAPTER 7

ON EVENINGS WHEN MOM AND DAD argued a lot, we knew it was time to get out of the way. Mother would be drunk and she would begin to argue with Dad, slurring cuss words at him, while Dad pleaded, "Honey, why do you get drunk?" A question like this caused her anger to boil over. She would attack him with her fists or with anything she could find to throw at him, chasing him around the house.

When they fought, he would run from her. Our father had become as afraid of our mother as we were. Most often he ran out of the house, jumped in the car and escaped, leaving us to endure the violence alone.

The truth is, our father wasn't around very much. He did work a lot, but he also liked to gamble and play cards with other Filipino men. He was gone far more often than he was home.

When mom drank with other men at the house, terrifying violence occurred. Once, a man pinned Mom on the floor in the bathroom, and he was bent over, punching her with his fists over and over again. Her face was bloody and she was crying. She grunted with each blow. I thought he was killing her. I jumped on his back trying to get him to stop. He reared back and threw me against the opposite wall. My attempts to stop him didn't work, but eventually he stopped before my mother died from his beating.

Mom became even more aggressive as her drinking worsened. While drunk, she often threw knives and anything she could lay her hands on. There would be broken glass strewn across the living room floor. Blood would fly as she landed a cut across Dad's arm or head, and we would silently scream inside, *Stop, stop!*

One of us would call the police, yelling, "Come quick, Mom is killing Daddy!"

And when we did, we would cry because we knew that meant they would come and take us away, sometimes for months.

CHAPTER 8

IT WAS A JUVENILE HOME. That's what my sisters called it. It had high fences with barbed wire at the top. It felt like a prison, there was no way to escape.

As soon as we arrived, they made us take off our clothes and shower together with other little five- to seven-year-old children. The boys and girls were only separated by a half wall in the shower room. We were given little tee-shirts to wear. I was embarrassed as we walked out in front of the boys. The tee-shirts only covered half of our bodies and even though we tried to pull them down over our bare bottoms, they didn't reach.

My little sister Lulu and I were put together but separated from the rest of our siblings. We were scared and confused. Often I needed to coax Lulu out from under the bed. She hid from the caretakers who wanted to brush her long hair. Our long hair continued to grow, by now down past our waists. They would pull our hair back tight, brushing hard and putting it in ponytails. While they brushed, Lulu's tears fell and I tried to comfort her.

The younger children were put in cribs, some of which were stuck high on the wall. To me, the kids looked like caged animals. I loved my little brothers and hated being separated from them. EnaKenty was between one and two years old. I remember seeing him when we were all marched through the narrow little hallways to lunch. He was in a crib that was pushed up against a window and as he saw me passing by, his little hands and tearful face pressed up against the window reaching for me. Crying, I stopped and pushed my lips and hands up to the glass separating us. But the women in charge pushed us along and wouldn't let me stay.

The only time we got to see our other siblings was at gym time. They wouldn't let us hang onto each other. We had to play games. I loved sports, but most of all loved getting to see my siblings for a short time. I didn't want the recreation time to end because we would have to go back and we would be separated again.

One of the times we were placed in the juvenile home was during the Christmas season. We all were in a Christmas play. I was happy to see the rest of my family when they came for the performance. Mom and Dad gave me a beautiful doll. It looked like Snow White with brown hair and dark brown eyes that opened and shut. I loved it! It was the first doll they had ever given me. I had it until their visit was done and then the caretakers took it from me, promising I would get it back. I never did.

We were brought outside into a small yard to get fresh air every once in a while. The time schedule was rigid, when to eat, when to play, when to sleep and when to wake up. It seemed like days blended into days. I longed for home and to see and hold my family.

I don't remember how long we had to stay there that time, but eventually we were all returned to our parents. Things at home had not gotten any better.

CHAPTER 9

Mom flew into a rage, more excessive this day than most others. Joyce, my second oldest sister, her target. Compared to the rest of us, Joyce was chubby and the only girl with short hair. She was a mirror image of Mom without the chubby. She looked like her. Her complexion was the same, and she had the same beautiful smile and voice.

"Fatso, get your lazy ass over here!" Mom screamed.

Of all the siblings, Joyce was the most cheerful, smart, loving, happy with a joyful spirit. Joyce, like Sarah, was a protector, too. She would step in if there was a chance to protect.

Mom was meanest to Joyce.

A few of us were in the big room upstairs with the giant closet that held all of our clothes.

"Joyce!" Mom screamed again.

I grabbed my little siblings and crammed us all as far back in the closet as possible. Mom stomped into the room. We could hear Joyce running up the stairs. She arrived in the bedroom, obviously scared.

"Mom?"

Mom grabbed Joyce by the head and smashed her into the window. Glass shattered and blood splattered the floor.

"You fat, lazy girl! I told you to sweep the floor!"

A gash spread across Joyce's head. She began quietly sobbing as the tears she tried so hard to hold back fell to the ground.

"Why are you crying?" Mom yelled. "Let me give you something to cry about!"

She grabbed a piece of board off the floor and hit Joyce again and again. Finally, Mom dropped the board and stomped out of the room.

Joyce had fallen to the floor. She was holding her breath and so were the rest of us. The little ones began quietly sniffling as I ran out to Joyce.

"Sh-sh," I turned back and cautioned the little ones, knowing if Mom heard them, there would be a chance she would return to hit them. I scooped Joyce up in my arms and cradled her. We continued to breathe deeply and quietly as I tried to wipe away the blood.

"Sh-sh. It's okay. You will be okay. Sh-sh."

I didn't have any tears and soon hers stopped.

We were all, at one time or another, the target of Mom's rage. Once she slapped my brother, Quinto, until his nose bled all over the table. She made me sit in front of them to watch.

She was yelling, "Did you tell your Dad?"

When he would not answer, she hit him again.

"Tell me!"

I knew what she was asking about, because I had told my father what she was accusing my brother of. I was too terrified to admit it, and at the same time ashamed that by not admitting it, Quinto was getting beaten.

Dad had taken me for a ride. To be singled out to have a special time with Dad was extremely unusual. He was driving me around, asking me to tell him the name of the man Mother was seeing. I was scared to tell him because Mom had warned all of us not to tell. But Dad was offering ice cream to me if I would tell him. Eventually I gave in and told him.

Now I sat there, like a stone. No tears, not moving, terrified. It should be me sitting in that chair with Mother's fist hitting my face, with my nose and lips bleeding. It should have been me.

We all had our favorite hiding places. When Mom went on her tirades, we would scurry to find a safe place to hide from her. One favorite was the small cupboard-sized space halfway up the stairs; it was like a side attic.

Often, one of my siblings would beat me to the attic. In a terrified whisper I would implore, "What are you doing here? You move over! I am not leaving," as we huddled in the cramped space together. No one dared leave as Mom stormed up the stairs. We'd sit very still while she stomped by, grumbling and muttering all the way.

The large closet in the upstairs bedroom was one of the safest hiding places. We could hide way in the back, hidden by piles of clothes. Other times, I would take the little ones out into the backyard and hide among the blankets that were hung out to dry. We called it playing tents.

34

FOR YEARS, MANY MEN abused my little sister and me. It was as though we had marks on our heads announcing we were available. There were times when we would be placed in a car and taken downtown. Our mother gave us to men to be used for sex. I remember during one such time, looking over at my sister, and wishing I could somehow stop the man from harming her. But I couldn't, because the same thing was happening to me on the other side of the room.

— Reflection —

Looking back, it's hard to imagine that neglect, domestic violence and sexual abuse became part of what I thought was normal life. How did I get through that? The mind of a child is not designed to handle those kinds of events. Something has to give, and a child, without even trying, will develop ways of protecting their mind in order to survive what is happening.

A clinician said I learned to compartmentalize the events and feelings of much of my childhood. He may be right. In order to survive the times when life was like living in a war zone, I had to temporarily store away my feelings, fears, anxieties, anger, and sadness into little mental compartments. This allowed me to not fully feel what was happening and focus all my energy on surviving the next horrible thing that was already happening. Had I fully experienced the emotional impact of what was happening, I would have been emotionally paralyzed, unable to endure the violence and abuse. So I learned to not feel the hurt of the words said to me or the terror of the violence happening in front of me. I learned to not show any sign that I was affected by what was happening. I used my blank face, I didn't cry.

During times of sexual abuse as a young child, I would stare out the window, detaching from what was happening to me. When I was older and still being abused, this same way of getting through those times continued to serve me well. During one incident, I imagined a small box, high on the wall on the other side of the room. In that moment, I knew I could "go there" in my mind, but if I did, I might never come back.

I even used my ability to pretend as a way to protect myself. I rarely cried, at least not on the outside.

A rainforest grew inside my heart from all the tears I kept locked in.

If I cried, Mother would beat me harder.

If I cried, my first husband would rejoice as he brought down more of his rage.

So I learned not to; I pretended. I pretended to not care, I pretended to be happy, I pretended it didn't hurt. I would pretend for my children so they would think everything was normal.

I would even say to myself, "I will just pretend that everything is alright—be a good wife, be a great mom, nothing is wrong in my home. If I pretend, you cannot hurt me. If I pretend and use my imagination, I can do anything or be anybody."

I would turn myself into what was needed for the moment: strong, polite, weak and frail, beautiful and arrogant, tough and mean. It placed a wall of protection around me that I wouldn't even be aware of doing. Just let me pretend. No one would be able to see the real me, or get close.

But there were times when my protections failed me and I would freeze, unable to speak, unable to move, unable to say "No," and unable to do anything about what was happening to me.

Protections we build on our own always fail us in the end. We think by setting up protections, we become invulnerable. That our protections will keep us safe. However, no protection we build on our own can be strong and firm enough that nothing, or no one, can pierce it.

One of my protections was to become a strong Christian, be the best loving wife and mother, then everything would fall into place and be perfect. I would become the woman of Proverbs, also. I would even go to work to help support my family. All the while, I was ignoring the taunting words attacking my mind and heart. The taunting voice that screamed "You will always be unworthy," "You will never be enough for anyone. No one will ever really know and love you, the real you. No one will ever meet all your needs."

These were my longings, and I wasn't listening to them.

They became a wide-open backdoor that no protection could defend. My attempts to get those longings and unmet needs satisfied would play out in destructive and hurtful ways for many years to come.

I can look back on the ways I learned to protect myself and be thankful for how they helped me endure my experience. There is strength in those protections and they can be used for good and they can be used to harm. We tend to take those same protections into our adult relationships as we get older. I see how I have used them in ways that have caused harm to others. But I have also learned to use the strength of those protections in positive ways.

CHAPTER 11

FINDING FOOD TO FEED everyone was always hard. The cupboards were most often empty. Many times, I made ketchup soup with warm water. If I found macaroni in the cupboard, I would get really excited, because then I could make a macaroni ketchup soup. We never ate full pieces of chicken. It was always chopped up into small pieces and mixed with something else. We never had a steak to eat, only beef sliced into pieces, mixed with vegetables. We rarely had desserts. Sometimes there would be homemade cake for birthdays.

At times, Mom and Dad took us to a place that had cans and cans of food. There were no labels on the cans, just the name of what was in the can: Peanut Butter, Corn, Milk, etc. We would fill up our baskets. It would be a grand feasting time at home, like a dream! I know now that we had been benefiting from a food bank that distributed free government food.

My dad sometimes brought home leftover food from the restaurant where he worked. But most of the time we never had enough food to feed our big family. Lulu and I often went looking for empty bottles to turn in at the store for nickels. We bought coconut, marshmallow filled cupcakes because they were the most filling, and we wouldn't be hungry for a long time after eating one. To this day, I do not like coconut-filled or sprinkled goodies.

Caring for the younger children often became my responsibility, especially as Mom's drinking continued. My older sisters were sometimes gone from the home, having been sent to live somewhere else. Sarah was sent from foster home to foster home. I never knew why. Joyce was sent to live on a farm for a period of time. I never knew why that happened either. It was never talked about.

The relationship between my parents continued to worsen. Dad came home unexpectedly one day and caught my mother in bed with another man. He began yelling and screaming, and the two men began fighting right in front of us. That man was the biological father of my four youngest siblings.

Mom and Dad separated soon after, and Mom won custody of all the children. We never understood that. Each of us, one by one, were brought into court and asked who we wanted to live with and why.

Mother had prepared us. She said, "You will be asked to raise your hand and tell the truth, nothing but the truth." I was afraid my hand was going to be too dirty to raise. Mom warned us not to say anything bad about her.

As I stood before the Judge, afraid I would say something wrong, I told him I wanted to live with my father.

Dad left and went to Seldovia, Alaska. I didn't feel abandoned when he left. I knew someday we would be reunited. He went to work in a salmon cannery and would sometimes send us gifts. Since he worked at a cannery, he once sent a whole case of canned money. He filled the cans with loose change, then ran it through the canning machine where the tops were sealed. It was such fun to open a new can because the contents were a surprise each time. They would either be filled with quarters, nickels, or dimes. Lulu and I snuck money out of one of the cans every once in a while and went on a spending spree, purchasing little puff cakes, candy, ice cream, and drinks for all the siblings.

CHAPTER 12

Before long, Mom decided to move us all back to Old Harbor, Alaska, to be closer to her mother. This decision fit my father's desire for us to live closer to him. Airline tickets for so many of us—Mom and the 11 of us children—were expensive, however, my father won enough money at the horsetrack to purchase tickets for the move. That flight, back to the place of my birth, was my first airplane ride. It was long and hard. I felt nauseated most of the trip.

Alfred, my older brother, was already living with Gramma, having been given to her before he turned one. This was not an uncommon practice in the Native community. I have one small memory of him in Seattle, although I didn't know he was my brother as he slept on the clothes in the back room in a pile of old laundry.

After what seemed like forever, we landed on Kodiak Island. I saw green mountains, green trees, and to my surprise, no snow covering the land. I thought of my dog, Susie, who Mom made me get rid of before we moved. She had told me Susie would freeze to death in Alaska. I realized then she had lied to me.

Our mother hurried us into a vehicle that brought us to a restaurant in the tiny town of Kodiak. The rustic restaurant resembled a big barn; dark wood covered the ceiling, walls, and floor. A friendly person came out to take our orders. I smiled up at the waitress and asked for milk.

She said, "Sorry. The barge hasn't come yet and we are out of milk."

I was eleven years old and thought she was joking. She wasn't, the summer barge to resupply the stores had not yet arrived from Washington State.

We continued our travels and all piled into a tiny floatplane—an old Grumman Goose. The engine was very loud. It sat in the ocean and as it took off, the water sprayed up over the plane and across the little window. We flew over the beautiful green mountains on the short hop to Old Harbor. The water splashed on the windows and over the plane as we landed.

Old Harbor is a small coastal village on Kodiak Island tucked against a lush green grassy mountain. An ocean strait separates it from Sitkalidak Island, directly across from it. The only access to the village was (and still is today) by boat or small plane. At the time we moved there, the population was close to 200. There was one narrow dirt road that ran along the beach. Less than 50 small homes, shacks, and huts were scattered around the village. They were built close to each other and connected by paths. Fishing boats were anchored in the ocean strait away from shore. Atop a hill sat a small Russian Orthodox church, with a graveyard tucked behind it. There were no tall or concrete structures, and the largest building was the school, on a small hill on the other side of the village. There were no electrical, water or sewage services in the homes.

As we looked out the tiny windows of the plane, we saw people standing on the beach. All eyes were on us as, one by one, we climbed down the little ladder out of the plane onto the gravel road. Children gathered and followed us up to Gramma's house, a tiny dwelling with four rooms. The living room also served as the kitchen. The bedrooms were filled with small homemade bunk beds with thin mattresses and covered with thin wool blankets.

As we walked through the doors of Gramma's house, we lined up against the walls and crammed together on a bench. The children who had followed us came into the house and sat down on the floor across from us. We sat in silence, looking at each other for over an hour. Then suddenly, as though given a signal, they all rose and left the room. Mom said, "Those are your cousins, they came to visit you." We all thought it so strange that they had not said one word.

Our family all slept in one small room. We would sleep head to foot, three or four of us to a single homemade bunk bed. Gramma, Uncle and Auntie shared a room separated from ours by a partial wall. Alfred, "Junior," my older brother, had his own room, being Gramma's boy. We were all getting acquainted with him as we didn't grow up with him. Our brother was a stranger to us, as we were to him.

At the back of the house, fish hung from the ceiling in a corridor to dry. I had never seen that before. I hadn't ever smelled anything like that either. The corridor also served as the storage and laundry room. We washed laundry by hand in big washtubs, then hung the clothes outside on a line to dry. We had no refrigerator. Food was stored and preserved in the storage room.

All of us took turns choking and holding our breath against the overwhelming smell as we used the outhouse for the first time in our lives. We were told to rip out a page from a catalogue to use as toilet paper, though the adults had real toilet paper.

A little building beside the outhouse served as the bath house, called a *banya*. Since there was no running water in the house, the water came from a faucet located outside the house. We carried it in by buckets for cooking and cleaning. We heated water on the oil stove where the cooking was also done.

I always felt like we were visitors in this house. It didn't feel like our home.

School in the village was easier than it had been in Seattle. I received straight A's and never had any problems with schoolwork. The problems I faced came from the other students.

Most of the youth my age spoke *Sugpiaq* as their first language, and English their second. The girls my age shunned me because I was half Filipino and couldn't speak the language like everyone else. Our speech was slower, our sentences had pauses. The languages of both cultures are beautiful. Although we picked up a little of these languages, we were not taught to speak them because our parents believed we would be more successful mastering the English language. My oldest brother who was raised by our grandmother is the only one of my siblings who is fluent in *Sugpiaq*.

I picked up phrases like, "I jokes!" meaning I was only joking.

They would tease me and call me names. One of their favorites was, "Filipino! Filipino!" It felt bad even though the words were true. "Alupuk! Alupuk!" was another favorite name they used. This meant "nigger," and they called me this because of my dark skin.

Most of the boys our age were attracted to the girls of our family. I didn't know it then, but we were all beauties—dark skinned, slim, and had long black hair that hung way below our waists.

Lanterns lit the house during the evenings. One sat on the kitchen table and one hung in the middle of the living room. Gramma would knit, and we kids would play cards or other games sitting in the circle of light formed by the lantern. When I got older, I thought the reason American Indian and Alaska Native people like to be in circles was because our ancestors all sat in a circle around open fires, or as we had, under the lanterns at night.

While living in Old Harbor, we lived the subsistence life, eating what the hunters and fishermen brought home, like duck, bear meat, and salmon. The women took care of the homes and the men provided for the family. We ate fish soup and homemade bread nearly every day. In the *Sugpiaq* home, the adults were fed first, children last. This was new for us. In the Filipino home, everyone sat down to eat at once and sometimes the men ate last, making sure everyone else was fed first.

There was no milk, so we drank tea and water. Cream, the rare commodity, was only used in tea, coffee, and the breakfast mush. Gramma introduced us to new foods such as seagull eggs, all types of fish, local greens and wild game, including bear and moose. Having to eat everything on my plate was a hard rule to follow. The first time I saw a fish head floating in a pot of boiling soup, its eyes bulging out of its head, I thought it looked horrible! We ate everything from eagle eggs to seal oil, fish heads, dried and smoked fish, fermented seal oil, brown bear and live urchins. To eat the live urchins, we picked up the spiny little creatures, broke the shells, and while they were still crawling across our hand, popped them in our mouths.

The barge delivered food and supplies once or twice a year, bringing all sorts of canned food: canned hot dogs, Spam, canned bacon, canned vegetables, canned milk, Crisco, canned butter, and canned corned beef. These became our diet for as long as they lasted.

I loved living in the village, especially in the summer. I could go and go, and never run out of new, beautiful things to see. Out in the field next to Gramma's house, I liked to flatten a small square spot in the ground and make a playhouse by using the tall yellow grass as walls, then pulling some up to use as a roof. I climbed the green grassy mountain that shadowed the village many times. I'd sit in the quiet on top of the mountain, looking over the whole valley. I knew we had big Kodiak bears around, but I never came across one.

Often in summer we children would grab garbage bags or pieces of old cardboard, climb the mountain, and slide down the hillside. In the winter, we would climb halfway up the mountain and ride pieces of cardboard all the way down the snowcovered hill and through the meadow to Gramma's house.

The ocean also became part of our playground. We swam in it and sometimes went with our cousins on a skiff to hunt seagull eggs across the bay. Near the shore, fish swam into a lagoon at high tide, becoming trapped when the tide went out. My siblings and I would take huge treble hooks and tie them to thick string. Then we would throw them across the lagoon and jerk the hook through the water, snagging fish. Many times we would proudly bring them home for dinner.

In summertime, everyone gathered food and supplies to prepare for the coming winter. The beach became a place of frenzied activity during fishing season. The men went out fishing and brought their catch back to shore. It was the job of the women, young and old, to clean the fish. We would sit together on the beach waiting for the fisherman to bring in a load of fish.

I learned how to clean the fish by watching Gramma. She cleaned the fish so quickly. She would tuck her hair in a beany hat that held all her silvery gray hair, then reach down, slice the fish open and pull the guts out. I mimicked her, taking the dead fish, turning it on its side, and gliding the knife across the belly. It felt both wonderful and terrible to grab the guts and pull them out of the fish. Then I took the knife once again and ran it up through the middle of the belly of the fish to take out the bloodline that lies just under the spine.

Gramma taught me how to knit socks and we made bread together. She made baskets, but not often. I loved simply sitting near her. She hugged me once in a while, I loved the feeling of her mushy tummy.

Uncle taught me old Native card games. I wanted to learn how to run a boat and shoot guns and hunt, but this was for men only. Women stayed home, washing clothes, cleaning, and doing the cooking. We learned to respect our elders, and be open and receiving to visitors.

No one locked their doors, as neighbors walked freely from house to house, entering to visit without ever knocking. We were always offered tea on our visits and something to eat like bread, fish, or dessert. Everyone would show up to celebrate births. And we all walked through the grieving and mourning times of death with one another. When someone was sick, we brought them food and drink, sitting beside their beds as they recovered. We lived together in true community.

— Reflection —

I lived in two cultural worlds, Filipino and Sugpiaq. I didn't know it while growing up, it was just part of who we were as people. Both cultures are soft-natured, with gentle tones and actions of strength. Both cultures are still thriving today, each in the area of their origin. Without the ugliness of domestic violence and abuse, living this life was one of richness and beauty.

Everywhere we lived, we were near the ocean, rivers and lakes. I would always be either in the water or fishing for what I could catch to eat. I played on boats and anything that could float. I swam the lakes and in the cold ocean water. I ran free through the land, climbed mountains, and walked through the dense forest. I felt connected to the eagles as they soared through the sky and felt like I could swim with the whales.

Today, I stand in the strength of both cultures. I express my cultural heritage through dance, dress, and celebration. Knowing who I am and where I have come from roots me. When I feel lost, I run back to these roots.

It is important that every event I am involved in includes fun, food, and connection. As much as possible, I am on the ocean, by a river fishing, playing, or just resting. I love walking in magical places where the trees are full and big with paths that seem to lead nowhere. I fly my own plane now, beside the mountain tops, and it always feels like freedom with much excitement.

It's a joy to celebrate new life with all those I know. And it is with deep connection I walk with those who are losing a loved one or with those whose time has come to pass on to the next life. Our children do the same with those in their lives. They are always willing to sit near a bedside, visiting people who are sick, needing encouragement.

CHAPTER 13

NEARLY EVERYONE in the village was Russian Orthodox. On most Sundays, our entire family would attend church. Entering the church, we had to be very quiet. Three small podiums lined the front of the church, the largest being in the middle, each with pictures centered on their fronts. All the people stood in the back against the wall—women on one side and men on the other—then filled up space toward the front, always leaving room around the podiums, and a path for the priest to walk across the wooden floor.

The Russian Orthodox priest dressed in a beautiful robe. He had an incense burner called a *censer* he would swing toward the icons and the paintings of saints hanging on the walls. When he would turn and swing the *censer* toward us, the adults bowed and crossed themselves.

My uncles were elders in the church and assisted with the readings. The words from the Bible were all read in Slavonic, so we never understood what was being said. A small group of both men and women sang the songs.

Lulu and I found it hard to stand quietly for the entire two-hour service. We would often get popped on the head for giggling or being silly. Many times we would find ourselves being pulled by our ears to the front of the church and forced to kneel in silence for the remainder of the service.

Even though these services were long, I loved attending. I loved getting dressed up, having our hair brushed, and feeling very pretty as we walked the short distance to church. I learned and read everything having to do with the church, memorizing all the things taught to us by our Uncle Senafont who was one of the elders of the church.

"I believe in one God the Father, Maker of Heaven and Earth and of all things visible and invisible."

I loved the singing in Russian and many times would hum along. The old women wore scarves on their heads and would bow and cross themselves as certain words were being read. I would cross myself when I saw them do it, but never understood the timing or reason why. We made the sign of the cross by taking our fingers with one hand and bunching them together. Then we would touch the top of our head, then stomach, then the right shoulder and then the left. At the Catholic church the same sign was used except we touched the left shoulder first and then the right.

I always felt the presence and awesomeness of God in this church. I learned that God was holy, big, unseen, but present. I knew He could see me and hear me pray.

I also felt the sense of worship from the people, who could purchase candles to light and place in large candle holders at the front of the church. Each candle that lit the room represented a specific prayer.

Mom often said to me, "Promise me that you will never change your religion." She gave all of us Russian Orthodox crosses to wear. She had sewn mine on a piece of cloth that I wore around my neck. The piece of cloth is the only thing I have from her. I have long since lost the cross.

I knew the visiting priest who came each Easter knew all my sins already, so I always prepared myself to tell everything when it came time for confession. Confession was required before receiving communion. Each time I went forward with one hand cupped in the other, facing upward, ready to tell my deepest darkest sins. The priest would give the sign of the cross over me, touch my hands, and say I was forgiven. Then I was able to go forward and receive communion. I didn't understand what it all meant, but I loved doing it. I knew we had to be very solemn for this serious part of worship.

The bread always tasted so different from eating other bread. In the Catholic church we received full biscuits and since we were always hungry we would gobble those up. Here in the Russian Orthodox church we received pieces of bread. I always believed the bread tasted different because it was "blessed by God" bread. The wine tasted like a teaspoon of sweet red wine.

Christmas and Easter were the biggest and best celebrations in the village. At Christmas, a procession of villagers carried a large homemade star from house to house. The priest led the festivities, singing and blessing each home. Women baked large yummy pies, and we were allowed to eat big pieces. At Easter, guns were fired in the air to celebrate the resurrection. I loved the tradition of going from house to house of the elders, trading our boiled, colored eggs wrapped in a handkerchief. We would knock on the door and say, *"Christos Voskrese!"* which means, "Christ is risen," and the elder would reply, *"Voistinu voskrese,"* meaning, "He is risen indeed." Then we would carefully unwrap our eggs and trade them. I learned many of the Easter celebration worship songs.

The villagers worked faithfully to preserve their heritage. They were devoted to, even protective of, the Russian Orthodox church.

A missionary named Violet Able lived in the village for many years. Violet is the same missionary who had visited our family when we lived in Seattle. She lived in a small house in the center of the village. We were forbidden to visit or go near her, but I would sneak over to her home because she had games and I loved to play them. Throughout the years, Violet Able continued to look like an angel to me. She had a glow about her, a kind face and felt very loving. Her quiet presence provided a safe place and a light in the village. Looking back, I believe this missionary's influence and prayer were responsible for most of my family becoming Christians.

CHAPTER 14

In the fall, after fishing season, life would change for some of us in the village. Money earned from selling fish helped buy food and supplies for the coming winter. It was also used to buy alcohol.

Immediately after the barge came in the fall, a long binge-drinking spree began. With the drinking came arguments and fighting in our home. Mom joined Gramma and the others as they all drank. Many times we children scattered to the safety of one of our non-drinking relative's homes where we would stay until morning.

When we had no safe home to go to, we witnessed the drunken fights between Uncle, Auntie, and Mom. Uncle would throw Gramma to the ground. The babies screamed and everyone cried. The fighting would continue until everyone passed out.

In the morning, the house looked like a war zone. Broken beer bottles and blood from the beatings trashed the house. With a sense of hopelessness, I picked up the empty beer bottles ever so quietly, while those in our home lay passed out in the same clothes they wore the night before. My mind tried to bury the memories of the terror I still feel from the blood being splattered everywhere as the adults punched each other, screaming out profanities at one another. Some words I had never heard before, but they sounded wicked and evil.

It wasn't a nightmare. It was real, it happened… Hush thoughts! The evidence is all over the room.

The broom made swishing sounds, mixed with the tinkle of broken glass, as I tried to clean up without making any noise. Lifting the babies, now silent as though they understood the need to be quiet, I changed their diapers and put on fresh clothes. Wiping their tear-smeared faces lightly with a cloth found in the pile of clothes scattered around the room, I'd grab some food, and take them into the tiny room where I placed them on the bed to feed them, smiling and kissing them all the while.

I had learned much earlier in my life to begin cleaning up as quietly as possible while the adults were still passed out or asleep. When they awoke, their hangovers made them mean because they felt sick. Putting the clothes in one pile, wiping the blood off the walls and mopping the floor as quickly as I can. Then I ran back to the children, trying to keep them quiet… hoping to make this moment of peace last as long as possible.

It would start all over again once they woke up. They'd be groggy as they staggered to the bathroom, then to get something to eat. After that they would begin to search for that first drink of the day. I wonder if, when they first start drinking and begin to feel better, they will come look in on us. They might even say something. And for a moment, life will feel almost normal.

Yet the drinking began again as soon as afternoon came, as long as there were still a few cases of beer left.

Many children in the village experienced the same thing, but no one spoke about what was happening. We would just go about cleaning and straightening out everything so it looked as though nothing had happened, only to relive the whole entire nightmare again later the same evening.

It was a wonder to me when I visited cousins whose parents didn't drink. Their homes were peaceful and the children seemed happy. I always wanted to stay in their homes as long as possible, to stay in the tranquil setting. I wondered if these parents knew what was happening in the homes where alcohol abuse occurred, and what they would have done if they had known. Could they help stop it somehow?

— Reflection —

The trauma impacted all of our lives, my siblings and I. All of us somehow played out what happened in our adult lives. Some of my siblings became alcoholics. I didn't want to be around anyone who became inebriated once we were free from it in our homes.

Later, as an adult, I discovered not everyone who drank, drank until all the alcohol was gone in the home, that it wasn't the norm. I could hardly get over the shock that people would have only one glass of wine with dinner or that there was such a thing as having a "social" drink without becoming drunk.

It was wonderful to find out there were people who married and seemed to live their lives without beating each other or having vulgar screaming fights. It was amazing to me to find parents who treated their children with adoration and love, with hugs and kisses.

CHAPTER 15

Soon everyone was gone except my four youngest siblings and me. My oldest sister, Sarah, was married and living in Kodiak. Joyce, for a time, went to boarding school, and then got married. Dad lived in Seldovia, 165 miles across the bay from our village of Old Harbor on Kodiak Island. He wanted all of his children to move there and live with him. So for a couple of years, I lived in Seldovia during the school year with Dad, and returned to Old Harbor in the summers to take care of the younger children.

One summer day while in Old Harbor, I went with my mom to my auntie's house for a visit. Mom was holding the baby, my youngest sister.

My auntie suddenly said to my mom, "Give her to me." She didn't just want to hold the baby; she wanted to keep her.

My mom said, "Okay," and she handed her my baby sister.

I thought it was a joke. But I soon found out it wasn't. Mom had given away my baby sister. I was heartbroken. I loved her very much.

During one of my stays in Seldovia, Mom had come to visit, asking to reunite with Dad. I told my father I didn't want her back in our family. We had restarted our life. We didn't have the cruelty and the shame of our alcoholic mother. Our friends could come and stay overnight, and we were safe.

Mom happened to be visiting in Seldovia when the Good Friday earthquake occurred on March 27, 1964, a major event on the timeline of anyone's life who lived through it. It measured 9.2 on the Richter scale, the most powerful earthquake ever recorded in North America.

When the earthquake hit, I was at my friend Dana's birthday party at her house. Dana's mom was standing at the head of the table, and I pointed out the picture that began swaying back and forth on the wall.

She yelled, "Everyone out of the house!"

As she finished the sentence, the first jolt of the earthquake stopped. Before we could move, it began again, this time with a swaying motion, coming in waves. We all ran outside.

Dana and I were looking at the trees as the ground began to roll. It felt like we were riding an underground wave. The trees swayed back and forth far enough that the tops nearly touched the ground. The other girls from the birthday party screamed and cried in terror. Dana and I thought it was the coolest thing we had ever seen, yelling "Whee!" as another wave rolled through the earth under our feet.

Later that evening, a tsunami warning forced us all to evacuate to the school. As we all crowded in and made our beds on the gym floor, the radio broadcasted the news. All of a sudden, Mom hushed everyone so we could listen to an announcement on the radio. The tsunami wave had hit the islands of Kodiak. Old Harbor had been hit the hardest, and everyone was feared dead. Mom began to cry. That was only the second time in my life I had seen her cry. The first was when she was being beaten.

We found out later, as the news all got sorted out, that it was not true. The people of Old Harbor had evacuated safely up the mountain. The only person who died was a man living across the strait who had refused to seek the shelter of higher ground. His body was never found.

CHAPTER 16

DURING ONE SUMMER in Old Harbor, Mom got sick rather suddenly and had to leave the village. I didn't know what her illness was. It was never talked about. I thought she left to go to Fairbanks to be treated and would be back soon. She left me with my three youngest siblings. I was 12 years old.

My aunt and uncle said I needed to be responsible for taking care of the boys since Mom was gone. With all my older siblings gone, I was now the older sister assigned with all that goes into caring for children, including taking care of them when they were sick. This meant I had to stay in Old Harbor for school that year as well.

Before school, I woke up early to feed and clothe the three boys. I came home for lunch and fed them, then after school fixed and fed them dinner, did all their laundry and put them to bed. I had already been taking care of them since they were born, so it seemed natural to me. It was very hard work with no running water and no electricity. Washing the dirty diapers was the worst, rinsing them out before washing them. I got blisters from wringing them out before hanging them outside to dry. To bathe the boys, I needed to carry water to the kitchen, warm it, and pour it into a make-shift giant tin tub. By the time I hit the bed, I was exhausted.

Mom and I wrote occasional letters to one another. In one of those letters, I wrote about my uncle and what he was doing.

It all started one night when I noticed my shadow on the wall. It was beginning to have a figure-8 shape. I swayed back and forth with my hands on my hips and giggled to myself. What I didn't realize was that my uncle also noticed I was getting a young woman's body.

My uncle began to sneak into our bedroom where I slept with my three baby brothers on one bed. The bedroom was not really a bedroom; it was only divided by a thin wooden wall that didn't reach to the ceiling and didn't have a door. We slept on one side; Uncle and Auntie slept on the other side. Uncle would reach under the blankets attempting to touch my body. I would push him away and tell him to stop.

I protected myself by placing my younger brothers around me. I arranged two of them head to foot in front of me and one at my feet, with me against the wall. When Uncle snuck into our room, I pinched them so they would yell out and cry. This chased him away for fear of waking my auntie.

So in this letter I took a risk and told my mother all about it and begged her to come back. She responded, "Please do not write such sad letters to me. I am very sick and cannot read them." So I stopped telling her.

Finally, I warned my uncle that if he didn't quit bothering me, I would scream out and wake my auntie. He stopped bothering me at night.

But one day as I mopped the floor I saw him coming up the walkway. No one else was home and I was trapped in the kitchen with no way to escape. He walked in the door and again I froze. I cannot remember what happened from that point on.

— Reflection —

I had become the full-time mother of my siblings with my auntie as the babysitter while I attended school. I didn't know how to be a mom. I was the oldest girl left in the home, still a child myself. The responsibilities I had to take on were too large for me and I felt the weight of trying to balance the emotions of the changes that were happening in my body, the responsibility of my siblings, and fighting off the abuse of my uncle.

I had my first crush on a boy as adolescence bloomed. He was my first cousin. In one of my most shining moments I saw him riding his bike toward me. I looked up in the sky and saw the first star was out. I quickly wished, "Star light, star bright, wish I may, wish I might, have this wish I make tonight. I wish he would ask me to ride on his bike with him."

Almost immediately, he offered to give me a ride on his bike! I was warmly wrapped and tucked inside his arms as he held the bike bars, and I sat on the boy bar in front of him. The stars were out and I knew I loved him.

Gramma and Auntie saw what was happening and forbade us to hang out as boyfriend and girlfriend because we were cousins. After I left the village, we continued to write back and forth about how much we missed each other. Then one day I got a letter from him and at the end he signed it, "Your cousin." I knew then our relationship had moved into strictly friendship in the cousinly-close manner.

One beautiful sunny day my cousins and I jumped in a skiff to go to a nearby lake for an afternoon of swimming. I got a severe cramp in my leg and thought I was going to drown but one of my friends helped me. As we returned to the village, there were many people on the beach waiting for us. We knew something bad had happened to one of our relatives. I had seen this before when one of the babies in the village had died and everyone gathered on the beach waiting for the father to return, who didn't know his child had died. My heart froze as I climbed out of the skiff. They were all looking at me.

My cousins followed me up to my auntie's house. It seemed many people were gathering there. I ran up the stairs and into the house. My Aunt Julia handed me a little piece of paper. I read the following short sentence written in pencil:

"Kathy's mom is dead."

I read the note and ran out of the room. I didn't know where to run, I just ran and ran. I found myself at the edge of the lagoon, all alone. I sat there for a long time, until night fell. I didn't cry.

As I sat at the lagoon, darkness settled in and I became chilled. Yet I remained tearless.

I wondered at myself, *Why are you not crying? Mom just died.*

I tried to sort it out.

Was I glad? *She had been so mean and cruel.*

Was I sad? *I didn't feel sad.*

Was it a terrible thing that happened? *I am now free from her.*

What will life be now without her? Where will I go?

I think I should be crying. I can't find the tears.

No one came to find me. I walked back in the dark.

– Reflection –

It would be years later until I grieved her, when my tears finally fell and I longed for her. It would be after my first marriage, wishing my mother was alive and wondering what she would have done had I called her for help. Would she have come to my rescue as I had done her? Would she have entered into the fight and tried to stop him? I needed her to tell me how to be a mother, what to do with my brand new little tiny baby girl.

CHAPTER 17

AFTER MOTHER DIED, my three little brothers and I left Old Harbor on the airplane to move to Seldovia to live with our father. By this time I was 14 and had never traveled anywhere by myself. When we landed in Homer, bad weather prevented us from crossing over the bay to Seldovia, so we had to stay in a rundown hotel.

A mean-looking, old man checked us in. He gave us a room in the basement, which had many beds. I sensed him to be an unsafe man, so I bolted the door, determined to not move from the room until morning when it was time to leave. We could peek out of a tiny window high up on the wall and see the feet of people walking by.

I put the boys down to sleep. Wanting to take a better look outside, I decided to move a chair from the corner of the room to under the window so I could stand on it. I noticed a large triangle-shaped shadow behind the chair, almost as tall as I was. I thought nothing of it, until I had moved the chair.

As soon as I moved it, the shadow began to move.

A giant clumping of daddy long leg spiders had been frightened into motion when I moved the chair. To my horror, they began to scatter, crawling up and down the walls and ceiling and all around the room.

I gathered all the boys on one bed and tucked the blankets tightly around them. As terrified as I was of the spiders, I was more afraid of the man at the desk, so I didn't tell him.

All night long I stayed awake flicking the spiders off the boys as they fell from the ceiling or crawled up from the floor. My fear of spiders became real that night.

CHAPTER 18

Seldovia is a charming village, a short plane or boat ride across Kachemak Bay from Homer. The highway cannot be extended to the village because of the large glaciers between Homer and Seldovia. Backed by beautiful mountains, the village captures the feel of living on an island, tucked away from the rest of the world of Alaska.

At the time we moved there, before the earthquake, Seldovia was in its fishing heyday with a population that neared 2,000. The town thrived on crabbing, salmon, and tourism. Fishing boats and skiffs filled the small harbor. The crab and salmon canneries supplied work for anyone desiring year-round jobs. The houses and businesses were arranged along a wooden boardwalk, built on pillars and just wide enough for a vehicle to travel down its path. If the vehicle was larger than average, everyone walking on the boardwalk would step over the rail and hang on until it passed.

A little hill we called Caps Hill sits in the center of town. The hill is covered in alders and berries. The small town also had a little K-12 school where all the children attended. Seldovia felt and looked like the ideal place to raise children.

When we arrived in Seldovia, Dad's place didn't have enough room for all of us to live there. Dad had a fisherman friend who allowed us to stay in his small home. He had one room upstairs and another large room we all crammed into as our bedroom. We were all used to cramming and sleeping more than one to a bed so that didn't bother us. There was a living room, a small kitchen, and one tiny bathroom. The friend drank a lot, but usually when he became inebriated he just went upstairs to his room. He and my sister Joyce ended up marrying later.

Since my two older sisters were gone, I became the oldest female still at home caring for my younger siblings. Now I had new tasks as a mother, except these siblings were older. I now kept them from beating up each other in fights, trying to watch over my troubled little sister Lulu who was already struggling from the effect of the abuse in her life, and being there for my older brother. I had to clean up the house, sweep and mop floors, fix and change beds, make sure all the dirty clothes were washed so there would be clothes for everyone to wear… In addition, enduring a new person to fight off abuse and making myself get up to go to school made my life a blur.

Dad worked ten-hour shifts in the cannery. My older brother didn't have chores at home or responsibilities with the younger children. Boys and men worked to earn money, and brought home meat from hunting and fishing. Occasionally they might take out the garbage. Thankfully, my father cooked and did the dishes, so I only had to make rice every day for kitchen work.

The cost of living was very high in Seldovia, and we purchased our food by credit. I went to work for the physician in town to earn extra money. My first task was to learn how to read his handwriting. Later in life, I found out that nearly all physicians had the same handwriting skills. I checked people in, took phone calls, and sent out bills. I also took on a babysitting job for one of the teachers who had three young boys. When I showed up, they showed me a pile of dirty clothes that reached from the floor to the ceiling. Part of my babysitting job was to work on getting this pile down. It felt overwhelming, but I still took it on. I was thrilled to receive $11 a day, which at the time was a lot of money for a young teenager.

In Seldovia, our family was treated with clear prejudice. Seldovia was a mixed community of white and adult Filipinos and very few Alaska Native people. Nearly everyone treated Alaska Native people badly, but it seemed they treated us even worse because we were very dark-skinned. I had one little white girlfriend who came to spend the night. I had just taken a bath and was walking out of the bathroom when she asked, "Why doesn't that brown come off when you take a bath?" One Alaska Native girl came to school smelling very bad, so I befriended her and took her home, helping her get cleaned up. What I hadn't realized was just "cleaning up" was not going to stop the prejudice. It did help explain some of the prejudice to me. Maybe some people saw us as "dirty" because of the color of our skin.

The kids at school threw garbage under our desks and none of the girls socialized with us, except my friend Dana. They picked on Dana because she had fuzzy blonde hair and she wore it long where it frizzed out. She was also extremely smart and a bookworm.

When I met Dana, our family was having a family picnic at the lake near the outside beach. She came over, plopped down beside me, and began to eat the potato chips sitting next to me. I would never do such a thing without an invitation. She began to chat and introduce herself and meet the other siblings.

Later, Dana and I got into a big fight in school during a basketball practice and she kicked me. I challenged her to a fight after school. This was a big deal. When students challenged each other to fights, they took place off the school campus so teachers would be unable to interfere. The entire school would show up to watch.

I waited for her after school and she didn't show up. And she didn't show up for three days! I began to feel guilty and wondered if something happened to her on the way home. I went to her house and her mom showed me back into her bedroom, where she lay sick. I sat with her for a long time, and from that point on we became best friends.

Dana loved to read. She and I would go to the library where she would pick out five books for herself for the week and hand me one. My love of reading came from her, as did learning what reading had to offer.

I entered the stories through all the books I read. I traveled the world, was presented in the courts of England, floated down rivers in the lower 48 by boat, performed heroic deeds, got away with high mischief, could fly, and perform miracles. We didn't have TV, so Dana introduced me to listening to Shakespeare while reading along in his books. Like going to the movies, my mind held all the images clearly.

Finally, Dad found a home for us to live in for a decent rent. It was on the slough and all of us were excited to move into this home. It was the most room we had ever had in our lives. The boys were separated from the girls and we even had our own beds. It felt gigantic!

There were eight of us living in the house, and when Alfred came in there were nine. He had quit school and went crabbing in the treacherous winter waters of the Bering Sea and fishing for salmon in the summer months. He would often bring home money to help cover our food bills.

The stores allowed Dad to charge groceries because he couldn't keep up with cost of rent and feeding such a big family. We lived with hand-me-downs from people in the village. I remember falling in love with a jacket in the store but knew it was impossible to have it. When Dad splurged and bought it for me, I felt like a brand-new girl.

Dad invited a friend to live with us. He would constantly remind us that this friend was a great help to the family. He would say how he helped pay the bills and without him we would starve. I still remembered scrounging for food for my siblings and myself in Seattle. I didn't like that feeling.

It didn't take long for me to find out why his friend wanted to stay with us and contribute to feeding this large family. His abuse began with offering me alcohol, small bottles of vodka. When I accepted, he would come into my room and molest me.

I started turning down the alcohol but that did not deter him.

So I began to stay out all night to avoid his abuse. I was friends with a young man who was five years older than me. He was one of the safest men I had ever met in my life, and our relationship was not romantic. I would spend some nights riding around with him and his brother. Other times I would sit alone on a hill, watching my father and the local policeman in his jeep running back and forth looking for me. At times, I spent the night at Dana's house and wouldn't tell my father.

— *Reflection* —

I feel bad about this now. It must have been torture for my father to not know where I was and what I was doing, whether I was safe or not. I believed I couldn't tell him why I didn't want to stay home. My mother had told me I was wicked. I didn't want my father to believe that too.

When I showed up in the morning, Dad would scream at me, saying how I was going to turn out like my mother. His words and accusations deeply hurt me.

I would scream back at him, "I hate you!"

But deep down, I didn't. I never hated my father.

Where were you Daddy?

Daddy, where were you?
I loved you so much,
But you were angry with me.
You should have asked me what was wrong.
I might have told you about your friend.

Daddy, you couldn't have known?
Your friend destroyed something in me.
I am still hurting from it all.
Daddy, did you know?

I love you, Daddy
And I remember your love for me.
I remember your sweet words
"Someday, you will be something"
"You are the one.."

CHAPTER 19

I HAD GAINED the reputation in school as the wayward child. I was the one your child should never stay overnight with. Father banged on the door of every house he thought I might be at when he was out looking for me. The police also knew I was often not home at night.

One night when Dad caught me smelling of alcohol, he brought me before the magistrate to try to set me straight. He threatened to send me away from the family to a place where bad kids were placed. I knew this would leave my siblings alone in the house without anyone to watch over them besides Dad. So I would "straighten out," and make all kinds of promises.

— Reflection —

I was sending out signals to my Father, to the school, to the community. I looked like a "wild child," but I was screaming for help and didn't know it. Had anyone sat me down and talked to me, they may have found out that I was running away from abuse. I was tired of being the "Mom" and it was too much responsibility for me. That I didn't know how to protect myself, nor my siblings and we needed help. Maybe I would have broken silence and said something.

I excelled in school. Good grades came easily for me and I would have just slid through school with little effort except that I challenged myself to keep up with my best friend, Dana. She was the A++ student, and I was second highest.

I walked with a confident flare. I was considered an "easy" target for the boys. I was known for running away into the night causing family and police to hunt for me, seemingly not caring that Father was worrying, trying to keep me out of danger and away from the wrong crowd. I dressed weirdly or differently than everyone else in my age group. Parents kept their children away from me. I was always in trouble at school for showing up late, doing silly things to the teacher or being disruptive in class. I was a ferocious protector of my siblings and would risk my life for family, friend, or pet. That was me.

It was a silent cry, and without purposeful intention on my part. Now as an adult, I realize that all my actions had meaning that someone watching could have interpreted.

No one asked if I needed help. My mother had told me never to tell.

CHAPTER 20

NOTHING HAD CHANGED at home, however. I was still the "Mom," still the oldest girl at home. And as most siblings do, we would sometimes fight. But our fights became serious, often fist-fighting, kicking, and pulling hair when we were mad at each other. Lulu and I would pull each other's hair and wrestle to the ground. Brothers punched each other and at times brother and sister fought.

One day my younger brother kicked me in the rear and I exploded. I turned around and it seemed like all the pent-up rage I had ever felt toward any human being broke loose. I punched and punched even as he cried out. I just kept punching him. Suddenly I woke up and realized what I was doing. I stopped and he turned over to face me. I grabbed him and held him close. He was almost as big as I was. We both wept in each other's arms as I cried, "I'm sorry, I am so sorry. I will never hit you again." I never did, nor did I ever hit any of my siblings again.

My little brother went to school with two big black eyes. He told everyone he had fallen down, but no one believed him and I walked through the school full of shame. No one questioned us.

— Reflection —

I had gotten a taste of the anger inside of me. It was a deep-seeded anger over everything that had been done to me and everything I had done to God and myself. This anger came out in all types of ways, verbal and emotional abuse to everyone around me. I could be tough, controlling, and even cruel when I wanted to be.

Dad ended up sending me to Kenai for half of a school year. At the time, I thought it was because he thought I was "bad" and he didn't know how to handle me. What I found out much later was that the principal of Seldovia had talked with him and told him he had heard I was being abused in the home. He told my father that if he didn't do something about it, he would have all the kids taken away, including me.

He sent me to Kenai to stay with the Seldovia principal's parents. They believed that if you trust a teenager enough, the teenager would be trustworthy. Unfortunately, I immediately gravitated to the wrong crowd, partying the entire time I was there. They eventually sent me back home. So Dad sent me to Anchorage for a semester to stay with my sister Sarah.

Then Dad sent me to Seattle to stay with his brother's family. My uncle and auntie had nine children: four girls and five boys. I was in tenth grade. I hit it off well with Norma, one of their daughters who was close in age to me. We went to football games, snuck out to dances on the other side of town, and knew all the bus routes. We were never afraid to ride the bus, even in the middle of the night.

Uncle Urbano wanted us to only hang around with Filipino boys and not really date anyone. But we liked "soul music." After all, it was the sixties. So we always wound up with the African American crowd. We learned how to dance with them, making good friends with the boys. One time, Norma and I rode the bus home together with our African American male friends. Uncle saw us get off the bus as we said goodbye to them. I feared he might hurt them, but Uncle just scolded and grounded us.

My uncle was a retired Major in the army. He always treated me differently than his own children. He would sit me down for hours, lecturing me about life. Most of it I didn't understand, but I sat in front of him while everyone else was playing or going about their business.

When I had visited them earlier in my life, my aunt and uncle lived on a farm near Tacoma, Washington. The first time I saw chickens butchered, I couldn't believe they kept running around after their heads got chopped off. I didn't eat chicken for a long time after that, although Auntie served it for dinner many times.

When Father sent me to live with them, they had moved to the northern part of Seattle. My uncle was the president of the largest Filipino association in the city. We attended many Filipino functions in their community. We attended big festivals and events, watched traditional dancing, and listened to speeches in big tents. It gave me a chance to learn much about my Filipino heritage and culture.

Auntie was the best seamstress around. She sewed the finest, most beautiful Filipino beaded dresses for the cultural events. The costumes had large puffy sleeves, made with the finest colorful materials.

Eventually, I wrote my dad and asked to come home. I told him the most heart wrenching story I could write—how I had changed, how I missed him and the family and my home in Alaska. He sent me a ticket.

CHAPTER 21

ON MAY 21, 1968, I attended a wedding reception with Dad. He never drank alcohol and didn't know the punch was spiked, so he kept refilling my glass. A boy I liked also attended the party. One of my girlfriends dated him, but she wasn't there, and he kept asking me to dance. We danced and danced until he asked me to go to his house and cook him some pork chops. But he wanted more than pork chops.

My father's words flooded my blurry mind while it all happened. Like everyone else, the young man thought I was a bad girl, and this is exactly what he thought I was doing on my nights out, so I didn't stop him. Angelique, my eldest daughter was conceived that night. I was 16 and at the end of tenth grade.

I didn't tell Angel's father until I was two months along that I was pregnant. He scoffed at me, saying, "I and how many others are the father?"

I broke my father's heart. Since the time I was a little girl, he had told me, "Honey, you are special, and you are the one who will be somebody someday. You will go to college and marry a nice college boy." Now, in shame, he again sent me to live with my sister Sarah in Anchorage.

At the time, my little sister LuLu also lived with Sarah and her family in Anchorage. It gave me great happiness to be with my sisters again. We all lived in an old apartment, with just enough food to live on.

One day, my brother Alfred's wife, Helen, and her mother, Tanya, invited me out to eat lunch at a restaurant. Before we ate, they bowed their heads to pray. I looked around the busy restaurant filled with people. I waited for Helen and Tanya to lift their heads, knowing they would be embarrassed. When they finished and began to eat, no fluster or blush existed on their faces.

So I asked, "How come you're not embarrassed, praying in front of all these people?"

Tanya smiled and began to explain the entire plan of salvation. Her words were filled with verses.

> "For God so loved the world that He gave His only begotten Son, that whosoever believes in Him will not perish but have everlasting life." (John 3:16)

> "For the wages of sin are death, but the gift of God is eternal life through Jesus Christ our Lord." (Romans 6:23)

> "If we confess with our mouth the Lord Jesus and believe that God has raised Him from the dead, you will be saved." (Romans 10: 9, 10)

> "Here I am. I stand at the door and knock. If anyone

hears my voice and opens the door, I will come in and eat with that person, and they with me." (Rev. 3:20)

She said that I could go home that day and pray, confessing my sins and asking Jesus to come live in my heart.

As soon as I got home, I went into the bedroom and closed the door. I got on my knees and prayed, asking God to forgive me my sin, letting Him know I believed He had paid the price for my sin, and asked Him to come live in me.

CHAPTER 22

FIVE MONTHS LATER, completely out of the blue, Angel's father showed up. I was shocked and pleased. He looked so handsome in his white shirt, but I didn't know why he could be here, visiting my sister's house. He said he wanted to talk to me. He disappeared into another room, returning with a stack of Bibles.

He said, "Place your hand on these Bibles and swear to me that this is my child." It was an easy thing for me to do, so I did.

Then he asked me to marry him.

In those days, a child born out of wedlock was openly called a "bastard." I knew this and quickly responded, "Yes." I believed it was the right thing to do.

We were married soon after in a church in Anchorage. I wore pink because I didn't feel worthy of wearing white.

On our wedding night, he held me and asked, "Is this baby really mine?" I felt my heart sink. I thought his proposal of marriage meant he believed me. Now I knew I would be living with his disbelief and distrust of me.

After the wedding we returned to Seldovia to live, but life with him was hell. He timed me going to the store. He asked me to account for everything I did, who I spoke to, why I was late if whatever

I did took five minutes longer than he thought it should take. He expected me to work and then took all my paychecks. He owned a truck, but never offered me a ride. Even though I was pregnant, he sent me to the store. I had to carry the groceries home without any help, no matter how big the load, even in the winter.

One day a friend came over to visit me. As we sat on my bed laughing and talking, I heard a sound coming from under the bed. I leaned down, pulled back the cover, and there he was, hiding underneath it. He would hide under the bed or in the closet space, trying to catch me doing something wrong. If a male outside the family spoke with me, he yelled at me, angry, accusing me of betrayal.

My siblings and I each worked in the cannery since the day we turned 16 years old. I learned to do almost everything there was to do on the job. Working in the cannery was horrible and fun at the same time. I worked long hours in the cold wet cannery while pregnant, walking home late at night, then cooking and cleaning the home. Yet, I loved working with the people. Plus, it allowed me time to get away from my married life.

We dressed in rain gear, covering our hair with a net, yellow rain hat, gloves, yellow rain jacket and pants. "We all live in a yellow submarine..a yellow submarine…a yellow submarine..," we sang and joked as we marched into the cannery.

In the little, dark lighthouse with the elders, florescent lights lit up the broken pieces of bones. We plucked the bones off the rotating table full of crab. Another job involved taking the leg of the crab and locking it down on a bar to hold it while the water blows out the meat. With a kick of the knee, water pushed the crab out of the shell, and a beautiful crab leg would fall onto the moving belt. We called this station the "blow line." Workers on the blow line wound up soaking wet by the end of the day.

The supervisors learned not to put my brother Alfred and me together on the task of gilling the crab. As two halves of the crab flushed down a long trench of cold water, having just been cooked with the gills still stuck on the shell, we swiped and pulled off the gills, sending the de-gilled halves on down the trench. We were so quick, we'd soon have high piles of crab stacked. So we'd jabber and laugh, every so often tossing some gilled crab down the trench, way ahead of the rest of the plant workers with their specific next task. Sometimes my brother and I got into crab fights, throwing the throwaway parts at each other, purposefully drenching each other on the blow line, teasing other co-workers and having much fun.

Cannery work was cold. The back doors where the crab was delivered stayed open. Flowing water used to move and package the crab kept the floors constantly flooded. Our job required working until the crab was gone, so sometimes I worked ten-hour shifts, ending the day in soaking wet gear. The cold caused my stomach to cramp and contract, staying constantly hard. The foreman took pity on me and tried to give me the lightest jobs and driest places to work.

CHAPTER 23

I BEGAN TO ATTEND the little white chapel in Seldovia, becoming friends with the pastor's daughter who was close to my age. As we sat out on the lawn one day, she began explaining to me how to ask Jesus into my life.

I said, "Ruth, I have already done this."

"What?!" she exclaimed.

She jumped up, grabbed my hand and pulled me into her house.

"Tell my parents."

So I described to them what had taken place in the restaurant with Tanya and Helen. And how I had gone home and gotten on my knees to pray. They were so happy and joyful. They said I should tell everyone in church the next Sunday. I didn't understand why they were so happy, but I did what they asked. Everyone in the church clapped and cheered.

I attended every service they had, Sunday morning and evening and Wednesday night. The Wednesday night services were called prayer evenings. And the elders did pray! We all kneeled and many times I began falling asleep as prayers moved from each person around the room. The elders prayed over our country, family, leadership, forgiveness, repentance, salvation, the future, the church, the village, and more.

I was eager to learn the Bible, reading as much as I could. I learned about the Ten Commandments, studied what happened in the Old Testament, read about how Jesus lived and died and rose again. I dove deep into the lives of the people of the Bible as I studied their journeys recorded there. Many of their thoughts and problems related to current events in my own life. I read about baptism and did it immediately.

I learned what being "in fellowship" with other believers meant. We were walking out our lives together in Christ. My heart overflowed with warmth as we shared the wonder of what God was doing in our lives. I loved that we never have to feel alone, how we have power inside us to strengthen our wills to do what is right.

CHAPTER 24

My husband did not attend the church events with me. I didn't attempt to talk to him about what was happening in my life with my walk with God. I had learned in church to just "walk the talk," and hope my husband got curious enough to ask or come to church.

I had finished working a long day in the cannery, had come home, cleaned house, then began cooking. I stood at the stove, making a dish taught to me by my father. Dad only cooked Chinese and Filipino food, so it was all I knew how to cook. I was cooking in an iron skillet, hamburger goulash with tomato paste and peas, a favorite of our family that we poured over rice.

My husband walked in the door, looked into the frying pan, picked it up, and threw it against the wall screaming, "What is this shit!?"

Shocked and angry, I yelled back. "If you don't like what I cooked, you can cook for yourself!"

He swung hard, smashing my face. I hit the wall and collapsed to the floor, smeared in goulash and my own blood.

I sat stunned as the realization overwhelmed me. I had married a man who beats women, just like the men who beat my mother. I had sworn to myself I would never do that. Yet there he stood, hovering over me, ready to hit me again.

I did not cry. I was afraid, not for myself, but for the baby I was carrying. I shoved this fear deep down inside of me.

Silly Girl

It is foolishness
What a silly girl am I
Thinking that I have
Something to hold on to.

Step backward
Silly girl.
Look and survey
What you think you have.

It is nothing—
There is no one
Who cares about
What you want or long for.

It is pieces and partials
It isn't all.
Why are you looking
And if you are—where?

Silly girl
Sit back

Become the dragon
And you will live.

There is no one here anyway
It's the only path.
Step back
With no mercy

Why have worry?
Who is there for you?
Who is completely yours?
There is no one.

Live.
Be happy.
Be content.
Do what must be done
Until your days are over.

So began my life of living with domestic violence.

It seemed the goulash incident opened the door to new levels of harm from my husband. He was quick to tell me what he didn't like about me or the things I did. The physical violence towards me started to come easier and more frequently. He threw and broke things he knew had value to me. If what he broke made a loud crashing noise as it hit the floor or wall, it served his intention to terrify me.

But he faced a tough girl who had survived worse. I first responded with defiance; I'd either scream or laugh. This infuriated him, so he would slap or hit me harder. I took it as though it were nothing. If he saw tears, he would rejoice as he unleashed more of his rage. So I didn't cry.

Instead, I pretended. I pretended not to care, I pretended to be happy, I pretended it didn't hurt. I would continue to pretend for my children so they would think everything was normal.

— Reflection —

Why did you see my beauty and then hurt me?
How come I couldn't twirl around in the room
And have you reach for me
In that way...that...unspeakable way.

Why couldn't you resist the temptation
Where you came to me with lust in your eyes
Instead of adoration and love?
It was what I was hungering for.

There is something strong about you
I wanted it, to protect me
To cover and watch over me
To stand guard over my innocence.

When you failed me
Something inside went dead
The happy light of my inner most being
It has taken years to restore.

Then one night after he tore up the house and beat me, I decided to leave for the night. I waited until he fell asleep and snuck out to my sister's house just up the hill. I had never told anyone in my family what was happening, and I wasn't going to begin now.

My dad and some of my little brothers were there and I didn't want to get them all upset by telling them why I was there. I just wanted to ask my sister if I could stay the night, but without saying the words. So instead of speaking, I showed my sister a picture in a catalog of someone sleeping in a bed.

Just then, my husband burst into the house and grabbed me by the hair, pulling me up toward the door. Dad and my brother both jumped up to prevent him from taking me. My husband turned on them and knocked them both to the ground. He dragged me out of the door by my hair and through the snow. I tried to yell out to my dad and siblings that it would be all right.

The next morning, I heard someone knocking at my door. I cracked the door open, peeking out to see who was there. I didn't want whoever was knocking to see my bruised face. My oldest brother, Alfred, dressed in his Sunday clothes, wearing shiny black shoes, returning from church. He shoved the door open and yelled for my husband to come out.

My husband came flying out of the bedroom. He pushed past me and grabbed my brother by surprise. They fought through the house, out the door, down the stairs, and onto the boardwalk. My brother, who was very strong, slipped in his new shoes and fell. My husband jumped on him and soon had his neck bent over the side of the boardwalk.

"Give up!" he screamed. "She is my wife and you are interfering."

My brother realized he could be seriously injured so he stopped fighting.

Later, I ran into my husband's ex-girlfriend at an event in town. It was the first time we had spoken since I married her old boyfriend. I asked her if she still loved him.

She broke into a wide smile.

"A deal's a deal and you can't give him back!"

She was right, I was trapped.

− Reflection −

Living with a person who is domestically violent brings constant fear of not knowing what is going to happen next— from moment to moment—when the one doing the harm is in the home.

An egg dropped on the floor,
a wrong look, tone of voice,
could set off a series of yelling, hitting,
or something being thrown across the room.
The sounds in the home are hollow laughter,
no singing or humming,
stealth movements from one area of the home to another.
Any music played while he is home is chosen by him.
A routine life where meals are on a strict timeline and menus are never a surprise. There are no surprise visitors who stay long, although they are so welcomed because the hope is that nothing bad will happen while they are here.
Public outings are timed and monitored.

The home is spotless and everything is in its place, all of the time.

Living in a semi-terror world, where children are present and some sort of normal has to be lived out.

Going to church, smiling and being happy while at birthday parties and celebrations as though nothing is wrong.

If anyone had looked deep into our eyes,

they would have seen the sadness and the fear that we masked with our light chatter.

Katherine's father at their Georgetown house

Garage where the children played at their Georgetown house

Old Harbor from the climbing hill

Katherine's mother with Sarah, Joyce, and Alfred

Seldovia before the earthquake. Her father's float at the 4th of July parade

Boardwalk in Seldovia after earthquake tidal wave.
The earthquake demolished the fishing industry there.

Katherine, age 10   Katherine, age 11 or 12

Katherine at 12 years old in Old Harbor

Katherine, age 13

Katherine in 8th or 9th grade with friends Beverly and Linda

Lulu (Axenia)
and Katherine

Katherine, in gold sweater, with her uncle's family.

Pastor in Seldovia who told her to go home

Cannery work

Gramma Axenia Pennijohn from Old Harbor with Angelique (8 months)

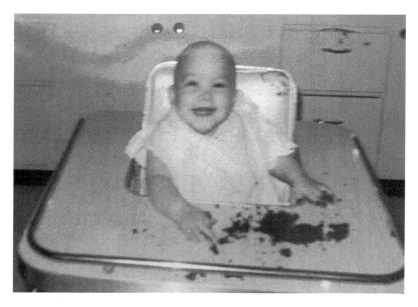

First child Angel while living in Seldovia

Katherine and her first baby, Angelique

Katherine's first two daughters, Marie and Angel

Katherine and Kevin renewing their marriage vows
Silver Salmon Creek, August 19, 2006

Katherine's family in her home, 2017

WITHIN DAYS OF THAT violent incident, my body began to ache and I had severe lower back pain. For 24 hours, I kept returning to the oil stove, held up my nightgown and rubbed my belly. Finally, I went to my sister Joyce's house, not planning to say anything.

She noticed I was uncomfortable.

"Is something wrong?"

"I've been up all night, standing over the stove rubbing my belly. My back has been aching me all day," I responded.

"You are in labor. You need to see the doctor right now!"

Joyce had a worried look on her face. I was only at the beginning of my seventh month of pregnancy. She took me to the doctor who confirmed I was going into labor. He had me flown to Anchorage. Joyce couldn't go with me. I was alone during my labor, 16 years old, and terrified.

One of the nurses, Yancy, stayed by my side. I felt like her baby. She'd sit next to my bed and whisper, "Uh-hmmm, it will be alright, uh-hmmm, it's okay, baby."

Somehow I made it through the long, painful labor. Immediately after Angelique arrived, she was placed in an incubator. I couldn't hold her, I couldn't nurse her, and I was miserable. I could only sit next to her incubator and look longingly at her through the glass. As a preemie, she was so very tiny, weighing only two-and-a-half pounds.

I cried quietly as I watched moms holding their newborn babies, and cried even more when fathers came bringing flowers, celebrating the new life of their children with their wives. My husband still hadn't shown up. He finally showed up two days later, although he had been staying in town with his dad and stepmother.

Before my daughter was born, I had prayed I would have a boy who looked like his father. My husband still didn't believe the baby was his. But when Angel was born, she had no hair, blue eyes, and even though very tiny, she looked exactly like her father, from the shape of her head and lips to the color of her skin.

Since the baby had been born premature, I had to leave her in the hospital in Anchorage while I returned home to Seldovia. She would not be released from the hospital to come home until she weighed five pounds.

For an entire month, I folded and ironed all her little dresses and outfits preparing for her homecoming. The town held a baby shower for us. Angel had enough clothes to fit her with a different outfit each day for a full year. I finally received the telegram saying "You may come get your daughter. She is now five pounds." I was so thrilled!

The hospital paid my way for the trip to Anchorage. When I held my daughter for the first time, she felt so tiny and precious. I realized as I looked down at her in my arms, *This little tiny thing is a part of me. I will have her for many years to come... It isn't just about a baby birth moment of holding, but will be a lifetime of living together.* To an unprepared 16-year-old new mother, these thoughts were a little overwhelming.

While the nurse showed me how to bathe my infant, she declared, "If you want to take her home, you will have to show me you are able to bathe and take care of her."

Because Angel only weighed five pounds, and looked so fragile, I was terrified I might break her. But I was determined not to leave her once again in the hands of nurses and doctors for yet another few weeks. So I showed the nurses that I could indeed bathe and handle Angelique. I grabbed her like an experienced mother and showing no fear, I gently but firmly finished her bath and dressed her. They released her from the hospital to me that day and I took her home.

During the early days of being a new mom, I missed my own mother. I wept, wondering if my mother could have shared wisdom about what to do about my husband's unkind treatment of me and his indifference to the baby. I didn't know how to be a mother, even though I had cared for my siblings. When I took Angelique out the first time, I bundled her up against the cold, winter air, and placed her in a little plastic carry chair. I lifted the carrier and my cocooned baby slipped right out and into a laundry basket full of clothes. I didn't know how to stop Angelique from crying when I changed her diaper and had already fed her. Although Mom was a cruel alcoholic, I longed to ask her what to do.

Angelique was a quiet baby and as she grew, I learned how to care for her. With the moon shining through the nights, I would walk and sway to quiet her soft cry. As Angel grew, she played much by herself, demanding very little of me.

Shortly after returning home with the baby, I returned to work at the cannery. My husband had no real job. I hated leaving my baby to be cared for by someone outside of the family, even though she was safe with a kind, good neighbor across the street. I often worked ten-hour days and my husband still did not give me rides in his truck. I walked to work and back, then often to the store with a baby in my arms to buy groceries.

Darlene, who had become my friend, worked in the cannery office. She asked me to work with her in the office and taught me how to do some of the light bookkeeping. I felt then I had my first real job.

The cannery supervisors took notice of me as well, and one of them often stopped and spoke to me in a flirting way. My heart responded to the flirting. It nurtured my life-long desire to be loved, held, treasured. For many years before I was married, I dreamed of lying in bed, being tenderly held by a loving husband who cared for me.

As I grew up, I would find myself looking at each boy, "falling in love" with them in secret, sneaking off letters to my sister saying, "Hello, how are you…I am in love with…." And each time it might be a different boy.

I never believed I was pretty, that I was worth being adored or cherished. I think now it was birthed out of my mother always saying how horrible I looked. She often called me an *Alupuk*, black in *Sugpiaq*, because my skin turned so dark in the summers. I had never met a black person before, so in my mind she was calling me a bad thing. Mother and Father never expressed that I was pretty or cute as a little girl. My mother made me feel disgusting and dirty, and she didn't hug or hold me. I was not cherishable. I already felt like that, it was just reinforced by her actions.

So how could any decent male desire me—damaged goods—as a mate? When boys chased after me, I always thought they wanted more from me than being in relationship. That it was only sexual attraction, because I wasn't attractive enough or have any sort of beauty that was worthy of attention.

When I looked in the mirror I saw a girl, not pretty, no beauty, just a girl. I didn't dress like a girl, seldom wore dresses. I was a tomboy. When I went to dances, I felt like a wall flower, even when the most desirable boy in our school wanted to dance with me. I assumed he felt sorry for me and would finally ask me to dance.

In high school, my long black hair fell below my waist, I weighed less than 115 pounds. Slim, I could wear anything I wanted and did. I guess I really didn't notice. I always compared myself to some other girl who was prettier than me.

See how the boys flock to her? And she is so pure and beautiful….no wonder, I would think.

My husband affirmed all my fears. He had pursued me for sex and married me only because I was carrying his child. All throughout our marriage, he commented on how ugly I was and how no one but he would have me. No makeup in the world would help my looks. I was stupid, not a good wife, a horrible cook, nothing like his mother (who was beautiful, by the way).

− Reflection −

During the single times of my life as an adult, I felt unworthy of men who pursued me. Always having in the back of my mind it was not my heart they were wanting. I never felt like a thing of beauty. Or a beautiful woman. I felt scarred, used, and ugly on the outside, with so much yearning on the inside to be loved for who I was.

There were times where I was singled out and felt a taste of what it might be like to be a "beautiful catch" for a man. But these moments were short-lived and didn't last.

I believe God gave me a beautiful being, inside. He has nurtured it and made it to grow. I know I am not the perfect woman, but there are virtues He has blessed me with. And more and more even in my golden years, He gives me fun peeks into my beauty, both inside and out.

CHAPTER 26

My relationship with my husband worsened as the years went on. By the birth of our second daughter Marie, our marriage hadn't improved. He continued his distrust. When I went into labor with Marie, my husband dropped me at the door of the hospital again. I was 18 years old.

Just before the baby was ready to be birthed, I began having trouble. They did an ultrasound and the nurse called an emergency. He told me they were going to have to do an emergency C-section. I didn't know what a C-section was. He sat on the end of my bed while they wheeled me to the operating room, holding the baby inside of me with his hand.

In the emergency room, a soft-spoken doctor turned my head toward him.

"I will be taking the baby through an operation on your abdomen," he explained. "The cord of the baby is wrapped around her neck and she cannot come out through the birth canal. You won't feel anything, we are going to put you to sleep."

The scurrying around and loud voices left me voiceless and terrified. There was no arguing. I knew my baby's life was in danger, and I needed surgery.

I awoke to find I had a beautiful six-pound daughter. This time my husband never even came to the hospital. He had gone back to Seldovia. I needed his support and comfort, but he didn't have it to give.

They released the baby and me from the hospital five days after the C-section. There were no travel dollars from the hospital to fly me home. My husband didn't come for me, so I had to drive myself to Homer. I was in so much pain from the surgery, I could barely press the gas pedal. By the time I reached Homer after the five-hour drive, I was exhausted.

I stayed with Joan, Dana's mother. She was furious when she saw my pale look. She immediately sent me to bed and took care of the baby while I slept through the night. Early the next morning I left for Seldovia.

Now I had two children to care for while working. And Marie was very demanding. When she cried, I thought the whole world could hear her. She wouldn't let me put her down. I found a way to place her in a baby carrier on my back while I did the dishes and cleaned our tiny home.

I was thankful that Angelique started walking before I had Marie. Going to the store and coming home with a load of groceries would have been impossible if I had had to carry both of them and the groceries all at the same time. If I were a few minutes late, my husband still questioned why I was late and who I had spoken to.

I tried to learn new ways of cooking, but he continued to remind me what a lousy cook I was and that I would never be as good as his mother. He found new ways to torment me besides his emotional and physical abuse. I was terrified of spiders and he knew it. He would lay a large rubber tarantula on the pillow beside me so when

I awoke, I would be scared out of my wits. He scattered small black rubber spiders in the laundry so when I sorted the clothes they would fall out.

One day I washed his favorite coat in our old ringer washing machine. When I put it through the ringer, it ripped in a way that I couldn't fix. I wondered what I could do, knowing he was going to "kill me" for ruining it. A friend of my husband's had been staying in our home. He saw my terrified look and asked me what was wrong. I told him my fear of what my husband would do. He said, "When he comes home, show him the coat and point at the washing machine and say, 'look at what that machine did to your coat!'"

So when my husband came home, I went directly to him, holding his ripped coat and said, "Look at what that washing machine did to your coat!"

He looked at his coat, grabbed the washing machine, and threw it out the door. I watched as the machine broke apart as it tumbled over and over down the long set of steps. I trembled, thinking it could have been me.

Angelique isn't able to remember the first eight years of her life. Marie remembers everything, like the time when her father came home angry, took me by my throat and pushed me against the wall, strangling me. He hadn't noticed that my little brother was sitting on the couch, and I was able to signal him to run and get help. He went to get our local policeman.

But as usual, before the police showed up, all the thrown-around furniture, broken glass, and ripped up home would be put back in order. My husband made it look like nothing had happened. I may have looked suspicious, but when the police officer asked if I was all right or if anything was wrong, I did not respond with anything negative. Though we lived in terror of the abuse for six years, no violent scenes occurred when we had company stay with us.

The church had a new pastor, and I was baptized during his time there. He was a very strict pastor. His wife did not wear makeup, and he didn't believe we should participate in dancing or any activities such as this. I worked up the courage once to tell him how my husband abused me. He said, "You are married 'til death do you part. Go home and be a submissive wife." I left that conversation convinced I had no choice. I trusted my pastor, but my heart sank thinking I had to stay in my marriage to please God.

After one violent episode, my husband left the house, our two daughters crying. I finally got them settled down and put them to bed in the converted closet that I had turned into their tiny bedroom. Right outside the closet door was our double bed.

When he came back in, I stood on the opposite side of the bed away from the children. I could see him in the kitchen through the open bedroom door. He had gone to a drawer, pulled out a large knife and held it behind his back as he walked toward the girls' room.

I stood frozen, knowing I couldn't run fast enough nor jump far enough to get between him and the girls.

He stood over them and shouted, "Wake up! Wake up!"

The girls were still sniffling from what had taken place earlier and began to mumble and turn toward him.

He continued yelling, "Do you love me? Wake up! Do you love me?"

All I could do was pray and watch.

As he stood over them with the knife trembling behind his back, the girls finally looked up and mumbled, "Yes."

He turned and walked back into the kitchen and put the knife away.

I began to plan a great escape. I knew it was time to leave. I knew we would never be safe there.

In the meantime, his rages continued. During one episode, he flung me on the bed intending to continue hitting me, but I had pulled my legs up and my feet were positioned to kick him, which I did, right in the stomach. He slammed up against the wall and fell to the ground. I got up off the bed ready to get slam dunked myself.

I yelled, "Okay, I know you're faking it! Go ahead and get up!"

He didn't move, so I rushed around, grabbed the kids and ran out of the door. I stopped them at the top of the steps, and we climbed off and hid underneath them. I told them to be very quiet.

Within a few minutes, my enraged husband came bursting through the door, ran down the steps, and left in his truck. We snuck to my sister's house and hid out there for a couple of days until his temper cooled down.

Then came the day of our escape.

I had purchased a small VW Fastback and drove it to work, pretending it was just another day. My sister had the girls, now ages six and four, and she brought them to the cannery around mid-morning, hiding them in the bathroom. My supervisor cut my last check and threw in a little extra, knowing I was running away and didn't have any money. The Police Chief checked out where my husband was and informed us that he was nowhere near. The ferry boat came in and unloaded and then began reloading the boat. After the last car was on, the captain blew the horn.

That was my signal.

I grabbed the girls and climbed in the car. We were the last to get on the ferry before the doors closed, the ramps were drawn up, and the ropes untied.

As the ferry drifted out of the harbor, I saw my husband's truck flying up the road toward our house. I had been careful not to pack too much so he wouldn't notice we were gone. I had even forgotten to grab Angel's shoes and she was barefoot. Yet, I knew he would soon discover that I was gone.

I looked out across the village and saw the small chapel and knew in my heart I was leaving this man for good, that I was choosing divorce. In my mind, it meant that I was also turning my back on God. I was taught to believe that divorce was never an option and would be a great sin. My pastor had ordered me to stay, but I chose to disobey. So, I took one more look and literally turned my back. I felt very scared, yet stubborn and determined.

Halfway across the bay to Homer, I realized with horror that my great escape plan had a large hole in it. All my husband would have to do is get on an airplane and he would beat us over to Homer and could be waiting for us on the dock. I didn't know what he would do. I thought he could and would possibly kill us.

I began to prepare my children, telling them how much I loved them and that their daddy may meet us when we get off the boat and would be angry with me. The ferry pulled in, and I didn't see him as I searched the dock. I took the girls down to the car, tucked them in, and locked the doors. We never saw him as we drove away toward Anchorage. We had done it, we had escaped!

I found out later that the policeman had called the air service manager and told him that if he flew my husband to Homer, there would be blood on his hands if something happened to us.

— Reflection —

I had dived deeply into a relationship with God. I had found Christ and was learning and growing in the spiritual realm while attending church. I had found a new connection with heavenly things and found evil was real. I believed there was nothing that would separate this newfound love I had in my Savior. So as I stood on the ferry, I heard the voice of the pastor, "You have to stay married till death do you part." I knew the only way I was going to truly leave my husband and divorce him was to turn my back on God.

As I literally turned my back while we passed the little white chapel where I had attended for six years, I felt the physical motion of turning—turning my heart, my will, pushing God away from me. I was leaving Him in Seldovia as well as my husband. I believed God would not keep me nor love me anymore for I was choosing to commit the grievous sin of divorce. I believed my pastor who said that there was no other choice for me: God wanted me to remain married. And as I had believed every other teaching received from this same man, I believed this meant the only way I could take this step was to turn away from God.

To me, this meant He would no longer be in my life, and I could not be in His. I believed that God would not be hearing my prayers nor want me to enjoy worshipping and being in His presence anymore. It was a profound and terrifying thought. But my determination and drive to leave overcame all the fears and doubts I had in making this decision.

CHAPTER 27

WE STAYED FOR OVER two months with a friend in Anchorage whom my husband didn't know. I didn't go out, worried that he would see me. Finally, I decided I needed to purchase shoes for Angel. I snuck out alone and went to JCPenney's. I had just paid for her shoes and suddenly, there he was.

My husband's father was a taxi driver in Anchorage and had asked all his taxi driver friends to let him know if they saw me. My husband asked if I would talk with him. I knew being in public wouldn't stop him from doing whatever he wanted, no matter what I said, so I sat with him. He was wearing sunglasses.

He told me he wanted to know what I was planning to do. He promised he would not bother us and that he would be willing to do whatever I asked. I told him I wanted a divorce and full custody of the girls and to never be bothered by him again.

If he didn't agree with me, I threatened to take everything we owned, including the shirt off his back. He had never given any affection to the girls, did not hold them, never changed a diaper nor cooked for or fed them. He never offered them a ride in his truck, nor did anything to show he cared for them at all. He did love everything we owned, his vehicle, my little VW, and a small furnished three-bedroom trailer. I told him if he agreed, he could have everything except the car I had purchased and now drove. He took off his glasses and agreed with me. He had a big black eye. I found out later that my oldest brother had given it to him.

He never troubled us again, and I went about looking to settle down.

We lived with my oldest sister Sarah and her husband in an old rundown trailer outside of Anchorage. The door didn't close completely and was held shut with a rope. There was a toilet down a long horrible, dark hallway with a blanket used as a door. Holes in the wood plank floor had been covered with pieces of tattered old rug. The walls were unfinished, and we placed pots around the house to catch water that leaked from the ceiling when it rained. Makeshift electricity wired around the house provided a means to cook and have some lighting.

Sarah had three daughters and one son. We did what we had done growing up, squishing into what little space there was. Wherever a bunk or bed could be built or placed, so be it. Children slept two to a bed, and I slept with my children on a mattress on the floor.

I was a single mother raising two daughters, both under the age of ten. Raising them on my own didn't feel any different than when I was married. Everything I was doing now hadn't changed much. Feeding, dressing, and caring for them all on my own didn't seem hard. It was tiring having to work, get them ready for the sitter, then come home, make sure everyone was fed well, tuck them in, and finally be able to rest. But that had been most of my life already.

With no help, sometimes, I would lose it. Lose it emotionally and physically. I would just sit and cry or kind of zone out and do everything robot style, without feeling. Television helps some now, if the children are interested in some cartoon or movie nice for children's eyes to see. There is always the worry when they are sick, really sick. Especially in the middle of the night, do I take them to the doctor? What can I do? They are not breathing well with all the stuffy nose illness, no medicine in the house, now we all cannot sleep. There was always the worry about paying the bills. Will we have enough for rent? Or enough for food. Sometimes I had to let bills wait, and I would get the notice that, "Your electricity will be turned off on such and such a date if you do not pay by the end of next week." Shopping at secondhand stores and going to garage sales seemed natural for all our needs. It wasn't easy being a single Mom.

— Reflection —

Just recently, while caring for two small children still in diapers, I was reminded how hard it can be for a single mother. Trying to deal with everything that normally happens in a home, cooking, doing the laundry, garbage, regular cleaning while working a full eight-hour day wears a person down. And doing this every day five days a week, with a hopeful weekend off. Although "weekend off" meant time to catch up with all the home duties that had fallen by the wayside because of no time to finish what needed to take place during the week. Single parents are pretty strong, physically, having to carry them, place them in car seats if you have a vehicle, or up and down stairs if there is more than one floor. Nothing is easy, it is busy all day and work all day, as rewarding as it may be to have children to raise.

CHAPTER 28

Iᴛ ᴡᴀs Nᴇᴡ Yᴇᴀʀ's Eᴠᴇ and we had all gone to sleep. In the middle of the night the phone rang, and I answered it. Someone was calling to let us know that my little sister Lulu was dead. She had been found by the side of the road, frozen to death. She was 19 years old, living in Seldovia, and had last been seen at the bar on New Year's Eve. Everyone there witnessed her very inebriated state, even remembering how she had fallen off her chair. No one had offered to make sure she would get home safely.

The funeral was held in Seldovia. So many people showed up they couldn't fit into the small chapel. It was a closed casket ceremony, extremely solemn and sad. People came up to our family after the service tearfully apologizing, saying how they should have assisted her in some way.

— *Reflection* —

Lulu was like my twin. We experienced so much growing up together. All the good and the bad. She was one year younger than me. We played, creating our own ways of enjoying the outdoors. We slept in the same bed the entire time we were together, shared each other's clothes, fixed each other's hair, grew up together. She and I had witnessed abuse happening to each other. When she was twelve she was sent to live with our oldest sister, with whom I was currently living. She had become pregnant and birthed a child at 13. We were told she had run away and gotten pregnant by a military guy who had come and gone. She soon became pregnant with another child and none of us knew who the father was. Lulu had become the sister who was a troubled girl, always getting pregnant. She was a troubled girl, but she wasn't a bad girl, she was being abused. We found out who the father was later and he went to prison for his abuse. Later she returned to Seldovia, married and had more children.

Her death was terribly hard for me. I still remember answering the phone and listening in horror to what had happened. For many nights afterwards, I dreamed of her popping up out of a grave, with a big grin, laughing, "I was joking! I'm really alive!"

I will always miss her.

CHAPTER 29

THE NEXT FOUR YEARS of my life, I found work here and there and began to bring home grocery money and even put a little into savings. I worked for Elmendorf AFB, civilian personnel, the personnel offices of both Indian Health Service and the Bureau of Indian Affairs. I had great supervisors who became friends. I watched how they supervised, trusting employees to do their jobs without micromanaging. I saw what the bureaucracy supervisors had to deal with while working for the government, the rigidity and hoops they had to jump through to make changes. I was responsible for logging in improvement suggestions in a book. These were never followed through that I knew of, so I always felt it was wasted effort. I learned how to operate and manage human resource documentation, track personnel changes, process promotions, terminations, career and tenure status. At some point, I got a GED for high school achievement. (Although I don't clearly remember when or how. I count this as one of those foggy, patchy memories of my growing up years.) Also, people encouraged me along the way to go back to school.

Eventually, I worked for the Alaska Federation of Natives under the Executive Director as his primary administrative assistant. When the Governor's office attempted to recruit me to work in their

Washington, DC, office, I decided against it and went back to school, instead working summers for the Wakefield Cannery. Joan Barnes, my best friend Dana's mom, hired me as an assistant bookkeeper.

Personally, I call these four years my time in hell. I believed God would not have anything to do with me because I had turned my back on Him from the moment I had left my husband and chose divorce. At the age of 21, I was free from anyone telling me what I could do or not do for the first time in my life. While I explored the nightlife in Anchorage, I experienced and did things that I had never done before. I had to learn how to drink alcohol because I didn't have much experience. I frequented noisy wild bars with loud music, people dancing, clouds of cigarette smoke and all types of alcohol. I played pool, and met people who partied every night. I found out Thursdays could be as crowded as Saturdays.

People who frequented the bar didn't only drink alcohol, many used drugs. The world of drugs was all new to me. I realized that I was naïve when I made the statement that drugs didn't exist in Seldovia and my friends laughed.

Nightlife in Anchorage was both very scary and exciting. Something new happened every time I went out with friends. I learned there were safe friends and non-safe friends. Having designated drivers hadn't begun yet. It was a miracle no one was harmed as we drove around in our inebriated state.

People "picked up" each other in bars, meeting people to take home for just one night. I began to stay out late far too often. My sister didn't like babysitting and didn't like worrying about me. She began challenging me not to stay out so late. She first asked politely, asking me not to stay out so late. Then when I didn't make any real changes, she tried a different tactic and said she would lock the door if I didn't come in early enough. And she did it. I found myself driving around in my small car in the middle of the night and even having to sleep in it because I had no place to stay.

Eventually the kids and I moved into an apartment I found in the Mountain View section of Anchorage. It was within my price range and it had two bedrooms. I could only afford mattresses, which we put on the floor, and a big round futon for a couch. We had a small, tiny kitchen table with a couple of fold-out chairs. Even so, we enjoyed having our own place. Eventually Dad moved from Seldovia and came to live with me. He became the babysitter. He didn't seem to be troubled or worried about the choices I was making as I lived out my single life.

Again the desire to be really known, loved, cherished and taken care of took me down a harmful path, through a series of relationships. I began dating and eventually found someone with whom I began a serious relationship. At first, I didn't know he was married and by the time I found out, I had deep feelings for him. I believed I was in love. I was willing to do anything for him.

This married man used me. He would be jealous and not want me to be with anyone else. He took the little money I had for his own drug use. He almost made me believe that I should earn money in any way because of my love for him. I narrowly escaped prostitution. I wronged my father and children by the way I behaved in front of them.

My relationship with God during this time was distant. He was never out of my mind, but I was not pursuing Him.

CHAPTER 30

THE RELATIONSHIP with the married man ended when I met another man at work who completely swept me off my feet. He was the captain on a boat called a tender. They would collect fish from the fishing boats in the inlet and deliver them to the cannery. He was the most handsome young man of all the men around, blond and very well-built. He made all the women turn their heads, and he knew it.

Whenever he came into the office, I found myself unable to speak, and when I could, I stumbled over my words. Eventually he asked me out on a date. I refused at first. But he pursued until finally I said yes. When we went on our date, I refused to go further than a kiss with him. This just heightened his desire and pursuit of me.

Eventually we became a couple and he asked me to marry him. We even set a date. He had called his parents and wanted me to meet them. His words were, "She doesn't look like what you might have thought your daughter-in-law would look like, but she is the pick of the litter." I knew he meant I was not Caucasian.

He was everything I would dream a man could be and more. He told me he would build me a home right near his parents and grandparents and we would all live together. I would be able to fulfill my dreams, go back to school, he would love my two daughters. This would all take place while he would continue to work in Alaska and I lived with his family in the lower 48.

I thought I was pregnant, and we would be adding to the family quickly.

God had a different plan.

I had let my sister Joyce know my plans to marry this man, who wasn't a Christian, and she began to pray, asking the small church to pray with her, as always, for her sister Kathy. One morning, after breathing this man's name every waking moment, I woke up and realized I did not have any feelings at all for him. At the same time, I found out I wasn't pregnant.

We broke up, and he was very unhappy. I visited him once more about a month later. I wanted to make sure I was truly not in love and that I could walk away from this relationship. And I did. It was over.

My girls and I moved in with my best friend Dana during this time. We lived by the railroad tracks with Smokey, our cat. We had a good life together. I had quit working full-time and entered college. Dad now lived in his own place and was newly married to a wonderful woman he had met in the Philippines.

One day I visited Dad and he was watching Billy Graham on TV. I said, "Turn it off, Dad, I don't want to listen to this!"

He ignored me and left it on. I thought it strange for him to be watching at all because he never watched religious programs and especially not evangelists like Billy Graham.

I plopped down on the chair, a little disgusted because I knew what to expect from the sermon. I had heard it all before. But he was saying, "This could be your last chance. This might be the only time you have to repent. You don't know if you're going to be alive in the next moment or the next day. Turn and repent. Jesus is calling you. You, right now." He was pointing a finger and I knew, he was pointing at me.

I knew God was talking directly to me through Billy Graham that afternoon. God immediately began to change me. He called me to radical obedience, turning my heart, mind and soul toward listening to the Holy Spirit.

The girls and I moved back out to live on my sister's property in the broken-down old house she owned. I was at peace. I began to go to church again, reading, praying and fasting. I found myself praying, repenting, calling out to God, crying and asking Him for forgiveness. And He heard me. I had been divorced for four years and away from God the entire time. Then in my heart I heard another call of obedience.

Go back to your husband.

So I went. I flew to Seldovia to search for him. Inside, I knew what it might mean to remarry this man. Images flew through my mind of potential future scenes, and I was not hopeful. But whatever the cost would be, I wanted to be obedient to God.

I went to the docks in Seldovia searching for his boat. I found him in the captain's deck. I told him there was something I needed to talk to him about. I was going to ask him if he would be willing to remarry me.

But before I could speak, he said, "Wait, I will be right back."

He left and went around the deck to the back room. Soon he reappeared with a woman. He said, "This is Anna, she is pregnant and we are getting married."

I congratulated him. I'm sure my feet reflected what I felt in my heart as I skipped my way back up the dock.

I returned to my house back in Anchorage, happy in the knowledge that God was once again in my life. I decided to buy some plants to put in the house. I had always had trouble growing plants, they didn't usually do too well. But this time they flourished and grew. It was as though they felt what I felt, a home filled with the peace and the presence of God.

CHAPTER 31

A YEAR LATER, I met a man in church. He and his wife had been divorced for a year. He had custody of his two children. The people in the church began pushing us together. The pastor was not opposing the relationship, even knowing we were both divorced. I felt that no good Christian would ever look my way because of my divorce. "You are married till death do you part," was still ringing in my ears. Although my first husband had remarried, I felt the guilt of him marrying because I had divorced him. Yet here was a Christian man who was interested in me!

My interest at first was more in his children than in him. I saw the girls and fell in love with them. I felt they needed a mother in the home to care for them. Monica would hide behind her father, hugging his leg while peeking out at me, sucking her thumb. She was four. The older girl, Tanya, was a proud little girl who stood straight, an intelligent seven-year-old. Our children's ages fit perfectly with one another. I knew he was intending to ask me to marry him.

I began to read every Christian book written on marriage and divorce. I spoke to as many pastors as I knew to find out what they thought. I didn't want to enter into a marriage and then find myself moving against God's will yet again. I had been walking so close in fellowship with Him throughout the last year.

I found a division, almost down the middle. One group believed that one could remarry with God's blessing, and the other argued that one should remain single always.

As I searched through the Word, I prayed and prayed for God to make clear to me that I could remarry with His blessings. Finally, I came across this verse, and I believed God was speaking directly to me with these words.

"If you forgive anyone, I also forgive him. And what I have forgiven I have forgiven in the sight of Christ for your sake. In order that Satan might not outwit us. For we are not unaware of his schemes." 2 Corinthians 2:10, 11.

These words freed me.

We got married at a quiet, intimate wedding with just the church family and a small group of our families and friends.

We settled in a small trailer in Anchorage. I thought it would be easy to blend our families. But it wasn't as easy as I thought it would be. His two girls had been without a mom for a year now, and Tanya, the older one, had taken on that role. It meant that she had "her house" in the order that she wanted it. So, when I came home and began to try to change things around to fit my needs, she was not happy. We argued over taking down her mother's homemade curtains to replace them with others I thought would fit better in the house.

Her sister was quiet but strong. She had a high threshold of pain. Once she sliced her hand and had to have stitches; she didn't cry once through the entire ordeal. We worked very hard, bringing her to a specialist to help her to quick sucking her thumb.

146

I gave them rules and directions to follow throughout each day or week. Then Monica and Tanya would visit their mother on the weekends. They would come back having had total fun with what seemed like no rules and lots of presents. Angelique and Marie, who were left behind, had to continue to follow the rules.

Although my new husband and I made decisions together, I was the major decision maker in almost everything we chose to do. I handled most of the parenting and discipline as well. I didn't know this troubled me until later on in our marriage.

I got pregnant immediately and miscarried two months later. The baby was a boy. I quietly named him David. I didn't know it sent me into a depression until my sister Joyce came to visit. She took care of me, cooking and singing soft melodies over me. While I was in church I came across Psalms 139. It said, "For you created my inmost being; you knit me together in my mother's womb." I began to weep. I realized I had been afraid to get pregnant again because I believed God would take this baby too. The fear disappeared after this realization.

We went to visit Seldovia a couple of times and my husband fell in love with the village. I longed to go back, even though my ex-husband lived there, because I thought it was an ideal place to raise children. We prayed about it and my husband landed the only job that had sound base funding. It was a maintenance and mechanic job for the City of Seldovia. It paid barely enough to support our family, but I chose to stay home to raise our children.

We lived in rented homes because we could not afford to buy a home. One of the first homes we rented was a house owned by one of the families in the church. They didn't rent out this home often, but utilized it to assist people who couldn't afford much money for rent. It had a living room, one bedroom next to a laundry room, a kitchen, and an upstairs bedroom. There was an oil stove for cooking and heat for the kitchen and back room.

The walls were paper thin. If we would have punched the wall with our fists, they would have gone completely through them. The way to get to the upstairs was through a door that looked like a wall until you slid it back and there would be steps. Once we had guests visiting and they were seated in our tiny kitchen. When I called the kids for lunch, some came in from outdoors, a couple came in from the living room and when several more came through the sliding door into the kitchen, the guest exclaimed, "You have so many children, they are even coming out of the walls!"

There was a tiny bathroom off the kitchen. The oil stove and a small wood stove in the living room heated the house. When the cold weather came, we could see our breath in the lower part of the house, as we could never get it warm enough. We had to keep the water trickling in the bathtub and kitchen sink to keep it from freezing up. It was so cold that the bathtub would have a chunk of ice created from the trickle of water.

We were thankful to have a roof over our heads, but when I look back, it was a death trap. It could have gone up in flames in an instant, and with our children living upstairs with no escape, it could have been terrible. After we moved out, the owners tore the house down.

I became pregnant with Timothy. I didn't want to have a C-section. The doctor had explained that since I had already had a C-section, it would be "very dangerous, but possible" to have a baby naturally. He supported my desire but said I would need to be in an operating room prepared for a C-section should they need to change direction. I was flown to Anchorage and had Timothy at the Alaska Native Service Hospital while the government still operated it.

We believe in circumcision, but the nurses judged me for being such a cruel mother, putting my son through unnecessary torture. The doctor was no better as I felt like he flung me mean looks as they made me stay and watch the procedure. I cried the whole time. I still believe we did the right thing.

When it came time for Esther to be born I had to fly out of Seldovia to Anchorage. I had planned in detail with a provider to have Esther naturally. This provider believed it was safe enough, even though I'd had my previous two children by C-section.

While in my ninth month, I stayed with my dad in his apartment. A window in his kitchen opened up into the parking lot. From there we unloaded groceries by passing them from his car through the window.

When I finally went into labor and was walking out the door to go to the hospital, Dad whispered to me, "Honey, it is a girl." He could always tell. I was surprised because I had always called Esther a boy while carrying her.

A doctor came in to see me and said my provider was not available, and she would be doing the C-section. I informed her that my provider and I had planned to have the baby naturally. She flew into a rage. She said it was totally unsafe and then said, "I will give you until I finish my lunch and then we are going to perform a C-section if baby wasn't ready."

I was only dilated to four centimeters. I needed to be much higher for birth. They didn't let women get out of bed at the time, so I asked the nurses to wheel me over to the phone and I called my sister. I told her what was happening and asked her to pray.

Esther was ready and was birthed within the hour, the doctor barely making it back in time to "catch her"! I delivered naturally a big, bouncing, healthy, almost nine-pound baby. After birth, I wanted to get up on the bed and dance! No C-section, no healing from the surgery, I could hold and hug her all I wanted.

Later, a doctor I followed up with in Homer was shocked, saying the birth could have cost both our lives had something gone wrong and should never had been allowed after two C-sections.

CHAPTER 32

Our church and the pastor's home were right next door. The pastor's wife would pop over just to come visit. She was always bubbly and ready to chat, and had a wonderful southern accent. She came over one day after the kids had left for school and I was laying on the couch. I was overwhelmed with the thought of all the chores I needed to do—laundry, housecleaning, getting ready for dinner, and taking care of the baby.

"I am overwhelmed with all the things I have to do today," I moaned, "I feel weary and tired."

The pastor's wife responded cheerfully, as she was walking out the door, "Well, get up off that couch and start doing something!"

I was stunned at her words and then got mad. So, I got up and began to throw the dishes in the sink, grab the broom to sweep, while reaching for a diaper to change Timothy. The funny thing was, the more I did, the better I felt and actually completed much of what needed to be taken care of that day. I laugh when I tell this story now, and I find people getting encouraged sometimes to finish their chore lists.

We went to church every Sunday. The kids all came home for lunch to a meal I had fixed for them, and I was always home to greet them after school. The older kids all had chores to do, cleaning their rooms, and doing dishes and laundry.

All the girls did well in school. I attended every single event they participated in, from plays to basketball games. I often volunteered as a chaperone or as a driver on trips. I was also leading the youth ministry at our church.

One time we loaded up the youth group for a trip to Anchorage. It was an icy winter day and we hit a patch of black ice. In what seemed like slow motion, the van spun around 180 degrees. Thankfully, no one was hurt. I got out to check the van and make sure everything was okay and slipped and slid. It was too slippery to even stand up! Eventually, we got turned around and continued the trip without further incident.

We had much fun putting up meat and fish when we got it. My husband hunted and we ate off the land. We formed a family assembly line to butcher caribou, deer, and moose. We caught and froze fish. Since we had a wood stove for heat in the living room, we took outings to find fallen trees. Then the wood would have to be chopped and put away.

I accepted hand-me-downs from everyone for the girls' clothes. People generously shared food and other items.

In 1971, the Alaska government set up the Alaska Native Claims Settlement Act (ANCSA) to settle their debt with the Alaska Native (Indian) people. Regional and Village Corporations were created, and qualified Alaska Native people enrolled as shareholders. As an enrolled Alaska Native to the Seldovia Village Tribe, I was deeded land. The Corporation voted to give all original shareholders three acres each, and a lottery was drawn for the parcels. I sold the land to use as a down payment on a nice, well-furnished home. We had a beautiful view. We looked over the top of a house across the street and could see the slough. Every day we saw bald eagles fly. Our house sat a short distance from the middle of town so we had little traffic. Our children were very safe growing up in Seldovia, and parents watched out for one another's children.

We kept the house tidy. After their chores were done, the kids were allowed to go out to play until dinnertime. We had sitdown meals of homemade bread and desserts each evening in our warm and cozy home. There was no alcohol or smoking in our home. We knew all the teachers personally and all the parents. With all four older girls playing first-string basketball, the school used to say if we lost it would be our fault!

Even shopping was fun. It was cheaper to fly the small commercial airline to Homer and purchase enough food and supplies to last for a couple of weeks than to buy small amounts of things we needed in the local high-priced store.

We loved to go on family outings. I had a saying, "Some people go to Hawaii and others raise kids." Not being able to afford anything expensive, we would take our little van with holes in the floor across on the ferry and drive up to Anchorage to have a couple of days there, taking in movies and shopping for groceries. Since seatbelts were not required, we took out a seat, made beds on the floor and bundled everyone up to go. We had many picnics on the beach and our children would swim in the ocean and explore the ocean life in the small tidal pools. We went fishing off the bridge, collected seaweed, and went clam digging in the wee hours of the morning. We put all of our effort, time, and money into our family.

We worshipped God and He was in our home.

As the children grew, I became more and more involved in the church and began to lead a youth group, as I had done before. I taught Bible lessons to the teenagers. God gave me words to share and taught me how to assist with each one learning more about themselves. The students began a prayer time at school and when the school told them they could no longer pray on school grounds, they walked to a place off-campus where they could pray. They led church services and learned to sing together. We visited other church youth groups outside of Seldovia, from Homer all the way to Anchorage.

I felt centered in God and fulfilled in life. Raising children and being involved in church ministry was very satisfying. I spent much time in the Word and in fellowship with Christians, living our lives out in Seldovia.

I loved being a mother. My children were God's most precious gift to me. But I began to be aware of some of the ways my own childhood impacted the way I was parenting. While I had not carried into my family the cruelty of my mother with the beatings and other physical abuse I experienced, I had brought with me the emotional and verbal abuse. It was shocking to realize the anger I still carried and the ways it played out in my marriage and parenting. My children were terrified of me. Just like my siblings and I were terrified of our mother. I had stolen their voices. I was repeating with my own children and with my husband some of the same ways I had been harmed as a child.

I controlled my children and ordered them around. I would not allow them to respond to anything I said when I ordered them to do something. Even if I was giving them direction or telling them something to keep them out of harm, they were rarely allowed to say anything in response to what I had told them. I ruled with a snap of my fingers or with a look that would kill. They would freeze and become instantly silent in church if I turned around and looked at them as they sat in the row behind us. My heart was broken as I realized the harm I was now causing.

One time my second oldest daughter said, "Mom, you won't let us stomp our feet up the stairs, or slam the doors, or answer you back. Is it okay to at least give you a dirty look?"

I was so shocked at her question, I said, "Yes, you can give me a dirty look."

She broke trail for her siblings, always stretching or changing the rules. She asked if when she came home and completed her chores, if could she then go out to play for a couple of hours. From then on, all the kids were able to do the same thing.

I learned not to ground them for too long because when they were grounded, I was grounded. When I did discipline them, I would make it fun for them to be home bound, but I tried not to make it too fun, since it was supposed to be a discipline.

I spent hours on my knees praying over my children. We would get into an argument, and I didn't know what to do to "fix it," so I would pray and ask for wisdom. My daughter would be in her room, crying, I would be in my room praying. It wasn't easy raising five daughters and one son. It was a lot of work, but I did love it.

I was the disciplinarian for the four older children. By the time my two youngest moved into the age where they needed to be disciplined, I turned it over to my husband. I said it is his turn. I regretted that decision for all time. They needed the same structure and discipline the others had received and it broke my heart to watch them struggle as they matured.

When the two oldest went off to college, it was very hard to let them go. I would cry every day when passing their empty rooms even though we filled them up with other children, I longed to hear their voices and see their faces.

Although the years in Seldovia were blessed and happy, my siblings and I also walked through some of the hardest, sad and terrible times in our family. We had all been deeply affected by the trauma of our youth. Lulu had died an alcoholic, frozen in a snowbank. One of my brothers had committed suicide. Abuse was still rampant in the lives of many of my brothers and sisters. At times, nieces, nephews and even my own siblings stayed with us for periods of time while walking through their own deep valleys. We walked through these difficult times, witnessing and experiencing the power of forgiveness and the beauty of reconciliation. We saw how God helped with difficult choices and how God could heal.

Life was full of busyness, blessings, and deep valleys during those years.

Beneath the surface of my own life, I was awakened to longings for a deeper relationship. There was an emotional void that was stilled unfilled. I still longed to be fully known and feel cherished. I wanted more from my husband than he was capable of giving. I wanted more in the relationship, more leadership, and deeper personal involvement from him in our lives.

CHAPTER 33

My husband had a desire to get more training so we decided he would go to school, and I would look for a job. That meant moving to Anchorage. It was a big decision.

We purchased a doublewide trailer from selling the home in Seldovia. It was located in Penland Park, so our cost of rent was the space for the trailer.

My husband saw the kids off to school, then attended classes. Esther went to kindergarten, the two oldest had gone off to college. The second two oldest girls were home before Esther and Timothy so they became the babysitters for the two hours prior to me coming home from work.

It was easier to save household money because we lived in Anchorage. Stocking and buying food wisely, we lived well enough off the small wages I was making from work. It wasn't easy, and during this time I became very sick. I was in constant pain, experiencing horrible treatment from the healthcare system of the hospital. We all entered the system through the emergency room, run through like cattle with case numbers and not names, and we waited up to seven hours at times to see an emergency physician. I ended up having surgery after seeking help from another hospital system. I vowed to myself to get involved someday to help change the way people were treated at the Alaska Native Health Service.

I began looking for another job, believing I had the ability to run an organization. I went to the CIRI Native employment agency and when asked what job I was seeking, I said, "Executive Director." The woman I was speaking to laughed, because I had a GED for a high school diploma. Later I would find out I had earned an Associate's degree but didn't know it until I checked how many college credits I had earned. But I had served on city and tribal councils in Seldovia, had bookkeeping experience, and managed and owned a small gas station with my husband. She offered me a receptionist job for one of the nonprofits of CIRI, called Southcentral Foundation (SCF). I took it. It payed $9.00 dollars an hour.

I joined a workforce of 24 at Southcentral Foundation as the administrative support person for everything. Filing, sorting mail, coordinating and scheduling for the two administrative people above me. I read everything that came across my desk. With my background in bookkeeping, I began to explore how the funding came through Congress and how it was used. I began to study the laws that impact Alaska Native health organizations and listened intently to decisions being made by the administrative directors and the Board for the population in our region. I learned along with leadership about self-determination.

As a receptionist, I noticed that people didn't dress up in the office, wearing jeans and sometimes even sweats to work. So, I began to wear slacks and dresses. It had a good influence on others and soon the staff began to change the way they showed up to work. Alaska Native and American Indian people came to our small clinics. I believed the surroundings, including the greeting areas, should be inviting and give a sense to the populations we serve that they were respected and worthy of the best. I replaced the black and silver government desk that would clang if you bumped into it, with a nice old used oak desk. Over cups of coffee I worked with the CIRI landlord to provide funding to repaint the walls and replace the flooring. It began to have a different flavor and taste.

By paying close attention to the finances, I found funding that would cover an Administrative Assistant position and brought the idea to leadership. They approved and promoted me to the new position. I hired my first direct report, the new receptionist. I then created and became the first compliance officer. Soon I was promoted to a position called an Associate planner.

During these years, I went back to school to finish my education. Southcentral Foundation allowed time for school, even to the point of my going to Hawaii to complete MPH classes as electives toward the MBA I earned from the University in Anchorage.

Before I knew it, four years after being hired, I became Executive Director, which was later retitled as President/CEO.

SCF began calling our patients, customers. And we were not only customers, but fought for the changes to become owners of our healthcare system. Always asking and always paying attention to the specific needs of the population we served, we stayed focused on what our customer-owners wanted, as we moved forward with making changes.

The years seemed to pass quickly. We grew from a minimal organization of 24 staff working out of a tiny rented building on a small street, to over 2,500 employees and many clinical and administrative buildings. SCF won two Malcolm Baldrige Awards, the only indigenous organization to have done so and the only health entity to have won it twice. Today, people from all over the world come to learn about our system we now call the Nuka System of Care.

– Reflection –

As a mother, I believed that going to work was a good thing. All the children were in school and the two older ones were able to care for the younger ones after school until we got home from work. At the time, it seemed like the right thing to do. But looking back, I would not have made the same choice. I realize that not all families have the option of having a parent stay home with the children, yet I believe children thrive when that is possible. I believe it is best for children to have parents with full energy for them, not distracted by work or anything that draws love, care and intimacy from them as children. My choice cost my children. This neglect plays out in their lives today.

I do not regret the lives that have been impacted for the good because I was placed in the leadership role of SCF, and yet and but...

CHAPTER 34

I BECAME INVOLVED ONCE again in church ministry in Anchorage. Although my walk in the Lord was strong, I felt that restless longing begin to creep back into my life. I started going out at night with girlfriends, innocently at first, just spending time with friends. Soon I found myself falling back into patterns leading down a destructive path. I felt alone, not known or understood.

The Struggle

I am struggling to stay soft
I'm fighting to be strong.
What am I to do?
I'm lost right now.

I want to grab what is hard
I am sinking
Shutting down
I don't like how I feel.

Doom is in front of me
I am fading
I feel the separation
It is happening.

My marriage started falling apart. I left home once for a short separation, but didn't want to go through another divorce. The feeling of hopelessness grew. I agonized about what to do. I felt myself go into a very dark and despairing place, between a rock and rock with no place to go.

Depth of Longings

I am deep in longings
I still want more
I still feel the greyness
I still feel the deadness.

Here I sit in it.
I've prayed. I'm looking for God
He is my rope
He can pull me out of here.

My vision is blurred
I cannot see
I'm overwhelmed with the nothing

The nothingness of life.

Dead, emotionless, tired
I feel the pull
Dragging me in
I want—I need—I want it now!

My heart is yearning
And I've no right
It is longing to hear
Speak softly, speak life

I need
I want
I long
Stop …

I decided to end my life.

I had a plan. I would step off a bluff into the fast moving tide and end my life.

There is a darkness that takes over the mind, body and soul, where reasoning doesn't connect to the dark thoughts that twirl around in one's mind. When I felt like I had nowhere to go, no "out" of the circumstances I was in, the thought of ending it all seemed simple. Everything seemed hopeless, no light at the end of the tunnel. Rather than putting my family through another divorce, rather than chasing longings in another relationship, my reasoning led me to think everyone in my life would just get over the loss of my life and move on. Life would continue without me. I am just like a pebble thrown into a lake, causing a tiny ripple before disappearing.

The day came and I arrived at the place I had chosen to take my own life. Just at the moment I was going to take the step, however, I realized I had left my journals in the car. For most of my life I had been faithfully journaling. I suddenly realized someone would find and read them. I ran back to the car and reached under the seat for them.

At that moment I began laughing out loud. I looked up and said, "Lord, you really have a sense of humor!"

Here I was contemplating suicide and right at the moment of choice He lays on my heart the thought that "someone might read my journals." I returned home, still feeling desperate, but grateful for God's creative intervention in my life at that moment.

— Reflection —

I believe spiritual darkness has a lot to do with believing lies and hiding truth.
The whisper of worthlessness,
of having no value,
that no one really cares and that this action is the answer.
The darkness is filled with a blindness,
a blindness to the impact suicide has on the lives remaining.
It's an uncontrollable thought pattern and without help leads to a terrible destructive end.
It is madness I know now.

But when walking through the decisions,
the madness cannot be seen nor felt.
There are always choices.
Choices in life,
choices that change the environment one lives in,
choices to change circumstances.
Instead of jumping off a cliff to one's death,
one can jump off a cliff that leads to life.

CHAPTER 35

I SOUGHT OUT a counselor. I talked through my thoughts of suicide and began the long journey of understanding the impact of my childhood experiences on my life. I had a true deep desire to be loved and cherished by God and my husband. And I was in disbelief that either really did. My husband didn't know how to love me and how could God love me when I was worthless?

It was many years of counseling before I began to believe that God really loved me, I was still living a vacant and unfulfilled life with my husband. I started attending a group that my counselor recommended. My heart became burdened for others who had known the harm of sexual abuse. I attended several Dan Allender workshops to continue my personal growth and to grow in my understanding so I could help others.

At one of the conferences I met a missionary who had been serving God for 30 years in Alaska. She shared my vision for helping those who had experienced sexual abuse. We talked about bringing a conference to Alaska for the Alaska Native people. At my church, I announced that I would like to lead a group in my home. Eight women showed up, all Alaska Native, and who had all been sexually abused. We walked through a 15-week Dan Allender workbook study.

I began to work for my counselor while he did his dissertation for his Ph.D. I did research about sexual abuse and helped administer surveys in churches about the topic. I taught myself how to speed read. During this time, the missionary I had met earlier invited me to speak at her church. I shared a little of my story, sang, and had people fill out the survey. I found some were deeply impacted just by answering the questions.

I still struggled with my worthless feelings, still had deep longings.

Longings

My heart cries out for more
The very fibers of my soul scream
for satisfaction.
My chest is heavy with yearning
And a void fills the air around me.
I am desperate to hang on to the life
you bring.
I am at a loss as to what to do with the pain
I feel deep inside.

Save me from myself, lest I lose sight of
everything good.
Free me from drowning
And becoming overwhelmed.

I cry out silently, nothing leaves my lips

I am soundless, but my being burns,
My thoughts are consumed
My feelings stretched to the extreme.

My counselor and I ended our sessions abruptly, sending me into a tail spin aimed back at *Does God love me?* Our family experienced tragic deaths. The timing of these and other events in my life once again left me feeling desperate and between a rock and a rock. The weight of my world seemed too much with no end in sight.

I was frantic for change, and I chose to get divorced.

The choice caused my children to suffer more than I could have ever anticipated. I had moved out, finding a place large enough to have my children with me. It was a horrible divorce, and I had entered into a new relationship with another person. One day I went back home and the children were all lying around the house like dead seals on a beach. They were lifeless, no tears, no words, nothing. Dead in their emotions.

I wallowed in guilt, believing God did not and really could not love me now. Living with the sense of being separated from God, not even having a peek of His light gave me a taste of what hell would be like. I knew the deep black of darkness. I understand how death comes through sin while one is still yet breathing.

The depth of my harm extended out to countless others who witnessed what I had done. Some believed because I divorced, they could also walk away from their spouses. Some believed sin was somehow free. But sin causes death, and I witnessed that. There are severe personal consequences to sin.

I watched the death of innocence. I stole opportunities for healthy strong lives for my children and unseen, unknown countless other lives that may have come to know the Lord had I stayed on the path. I realize that people are responsible for their own actions. I also know God says if we harm one of these, it is better that a millstone be tied around our necks and be drowned. He says we will be accountable and will have to give account for all we have done. The Lord says that our sins are passed down from generation to generation. But He also says He relents.

CHAPTER 36

Two YEARS LATER I remarried. My husband and I had been working together for nearly ten years. It wasn't a recognized love that came overnight with him. First it was a growing deep relationship. His care and gentle ways of communication felt safe. When I went into crisis with my family he was there. When I became sick he was there. When I had major neck surgery before we were married, he came to my room to visit. I dreamt he whispered to me that he loved me. Years later I asked him about this and he asked, "Were you awake?"

He was the behind-the-scenes support person at work, fixing problems I had with those in power who could have made decisions I was making difficult. He hovered over me without my notice, watching for places where he could step in to smooth over a conversation that may have not gone smoothly with a co-worker.

He became my number one consultant in matters at work that I thought might not have any solutions. He was a major asset in problem solving. We began to spend more and more hours together in long discussions of the future, in both our personal and professional lives. My trust in his wisdom grew as did my feelings for him. We both seemed to realize at the same time that we had fallen in love, seriously enough to marry.

We let our Board of Directors know we were becoming more serious in our relationship and offered for one of us to resign. The Board would have none of it and placed us both under contract directly to them.

Kevin

He really loves me.

His ways of loving me,
Always a surprise and unexpected.
As though he read my mind
And really knew me.

Troubled in my heart with turmoil in my thoughts,
He would reach over and gently touch my hand.
Surprised, I would feel the turmoil leave
And a flood of sweet peace come over me.

Angry and frustrated
Determined not to discuss the problem
Traveling in silence in the car
Mind reeling in sadness of feeling misunderstood.

He stops the car
Pulls into a park covered in grass
Lays me on the ground and covering me

He asked, "What is troubling you?"

Climbing into my big van
I didn't notice my passengers
Suddenly in the back window
There they were, two large stuffed bears.

He had purchased them,
Strapping them into their seats
There to greet me
As though to say, "He really loves you."

Stability and strength
Never swaying nor running
From me as I struggled with longings
To be known, cherished and loved.

He really loves me.

We entered marriage, with one dog, six children, some already with their own families. He patiently built relationships with them and the grandchildren. He inherited my large family with ten living siblings, their families, and extended family.

Life has been a roller coaster ride for us, growing together in the maturity of our marriage, being parents of a blended family and growing a large organization. We have had ups and downs like all families and marriages. He has proven to be a man of high integrity, courage, and he has been my warrior. He fights for me and for our children. Almost all of our children have come to live with us one time or another. Once we had more than ten of them living under our roof at one time. Kevin built bunk beds where the children would have a place to sleep all together. I am not sure if they felt squished. They seemed very happy and content.

He is Grandpa to all of them. Playing and joining together in all the outings. Making space for them to live out life with us. He interacts with them and teases relentlessly. When all of them are over, he connects with the men, standing off into a corner with them, visiting while the children play loudly, covering almost every inch of our small living and dining room.

He fixes everything and is there whenever one of them asks for help. There is no jealousy with his love, he loves well. He has made our home a safe haven for all of us.

Soon after we were married, Kevin suggested we go to church. I told him I didn't know how to worship God anymore. Though I knew I was forgiven, I struggled.

But, at his strong urging, we went. We sat way in the back of the church. The pastor got up to speak and the first thing he said was, "Welcome, just the fact that you have entered these doors is an act of worship."

We attended church faithfully. I didn't volunteer for anything, feeling I was unworthy, sure I would only fail Him again if I did.

For five years, I prayed I would again hear His voice. In time past, He had often spoken to me through His Word. A verse would jump off the page right into my lap, and I would know it was Him speaking directly to me. Sometimes it was through a person saying something to me.

Once I was walking home late one dark starry evening, feeling rejected and unloved. I looked up and saw a comet soaring through the sky and a loud voice with it, "I love you!" I knew it was the voice of God. It wasn't until years later when I was sharing this story to someone living in the village and he said, "I remember that night. I saw that comet." No one else had witnessed it when I had asked about it at the time.

— Reflection —

Being a Christian is to know Jesus. It is being in a relationship with Him, with God. Relationship is having and hearing the Holy Spirit inside of me, leading and guiding, never feeling alone, always knowing there is someone very powerful watching over me. It's reading the Bible and hearing God speak through the words of the pages, specific statements meant for my eyes to see and my soul to receive. It is feeling like standing in the warmth of the sunshine even when it isn't out, even when it is night. It is sleeping in peace no matter what the circumstances are in life.

I had known tastes of this. I knew what I was missing because I had experienced all of this many times in my past daily life. I wanted it back again. There was a giant hole in my life.

I was sitting with Gail, a dear Christian friend at a club where many of us would gather for a glass of wine after work.

I confessed to her, "I would give up anything, even my husband, if only I could have a relationship with God again."

She said, "You are believing a lie, Katherine! Jesus died for all your sins, you are forgiven and you are His child!"

Then one Sunday while sitting in church, I began turning to a scripture the pastor was speaking about. Instead I found myself reading:

> "And the God of all grace, who called you to His eternal glory in Christ, after you have suffered a little while, will himself restore you and make you strong, firm and steadfast. To Him be the power for ever and ever. Amen." 1 Peter 5:10

And I knew. I began crying. God had spoken to me! He spoke to me! It had been a silent, agonizing five years.

CHAPTER 37

THE VERY NEXT MORNING, the missionary I had met at the Dan Allender conference was sitting in my office. I was surprised to see her because it had been five years since we'd seen each other last.

She said, "Do you still want to bring a Christian conference to Alaska to address child sexual abuse? I have been all over Alaska asking churches to help and have not received any support. I know SCF is a secular organization, but would you be willing?"

"Yes!" I responded without any hesitation. I was so excited. It was another affirmation. God was restoring and using me!

I had recently attended a meeting where a presentation was given about how much domestic violence and child maltreatment was happening in Alaska. At the end of the presentation an Alaska Native tribal doctor told her story of rape. About thirty hospital administrators and doctors filled the room. The audience sat in stunned silence as the impact of her story and the data had time to settle. Her story confirmed in my heart the need to bring a program to our state that would respond to the devastation of domestic violence, child sexual abuse, and neglect. I went to the SCF Board of Directors and gained permission to begin the faith-based initiative within the organization.

I formed a steering committee made up of people with the same passion born of their faith. Several Alaska Native people and a couple of master's level clinicians joined us to begin our search. We traveled across the country attending workshops on child maltreatment and child sexual abuse. My missionary friend found one called Survivors of Abuse Leadership Training Seminar (SALTS), based in Michigan.

We all went to the workshop to "assess the program." The curriculum weaved Christ throughout the entire week. Here, I told my entire story of harm. Until that week, I hadn't told my complete story of sexual abuse and domestic violence.

I wept uncontrollably while the group walked through every part of my story with me. They allowed me to share bits and pieces of my trauma through my tears, then responded in love, covering my shame and lifting me up and out of the depths of my grief.

Everyone on our committee loved the conference and decided to come back through another time. We brought other people outside of the committee with us to help us truly assess the program. The second time through led me to an understanding of the harm I had caused. I grieved and wept the whole week for the harm to my family, friends, co-workers and those I had relationships with in life. Again, the group walked through the weeklong journey with me.

During the week, I was deep into devotional and praying time, seeking God's voice and direction for my life. During an especially difficult part of the conference, I took a walk along a path leading to Lake Michigan. I asked God to speak to me.

I strolled along the beach and listened to the waves roll. They reminded me of the ocean. Finding a place to rest, I sat down and the sun became so bright that even though I had sunglasses on, I had to close my eyes. It seemed as though I was covered in holiness, and I slipped off my shoes.

After a time of basking in the brilliance, I rose and began to walk again along the beach. I felt like God was saying "Look behind you." I turned and saw many trees along the shoreline. "These are people, thousands of people. You will lead them. Just as I called Moses, I am calling you to do the same."

I believe He was using the example of Moses to give me direction for my life in this new ministry. I literally laughed out loud. *Me? Moses?*

Again, when that week was over, I had changed.

I went to visit one of my daughters right after the workshop, realizing God was calling me to take steps of restoration for the harm I had done. No one had suggested I should do this. I sat down with my daughter and told her about the conference. I then said to her, "I know I have harmed you, and I want to tell you how. I am not asking for forgiveness but asking that you listen. Then you have my blessing to say anything you want, ask any questions, be angry and/ or be sad. Anytime, even long after we have this talk, if something comes to your mind and you want to talk with me about it, I am open to this."

I told her I was guilty of harming her and her siblings with emotional and verbal abuse in the way I had raised them. I confessed I realized how I had stolen their voices and raised them to fear me.

We cried together while we talked through times I had done things to shame her and her siblings. We went to bed exhausted, and the next day she spoke to me about things she remembered. It was a healing time for both of us.

Reconciliation With Children

What? Why are you whispering?
Say it a little louder!
What's wrong with you?
What do you mean I harmed you?

Stole your voice?
Who me?
I only tried to teach you right from wrong.
Don't give me that nonsense.

Wait, wait.. you do whisper.
And shy away from saying what you need.
I did that to you?
My tone? My looks? My anger?

Come, no, please come here.
Listen, I am so sorry.
I love you and hate what I have done.
Come…let's talk.

When I had realized all the harm I had done with my children and decided to talk with each one, it was not an easy thing to do. I had to wait and make sure the timing was right. I have gone to each one, and all of them know even now, that when they are ready, I am willing to walk through their stories with each one.

It wasn't forgiveness that I was asking for. It was a giant attempt to acknowledge my harm and help restore their voices I had stolen. It was to help them understand the impact of my harm in their lives and help them to recognize the consequences of my actions. I wanted them to think about how my harm may be impacting their own lives today. How do they speak with their children? Are they mimicking anything I have done now with their own families? Or friends? Are their tones liken to mine? Are they shutting their children down, stealing their voices?

They all have risen up and called me blessed. They all love me, I know. Some have voiced that they have forgiven me. It has opened our lives to one another in a deeper more meaningful way. We speak to one another better. Our relationship is closer.

CHAPTER 38

I WENT BEFORE tribal leadership, the Alaska Federation of Natives and the Alaska Native Health Board to present this new initiative. Our committee came back excited to begin the work of ending domestic violence, child sexual abuse, and child neglect. The reception was less than enthusiastic, especially from the men.

I wondered about this until I had a conversation with a person from one of the foundations we were speaking with.

He asked me, "Have you ever studied what happened in the early 60s with the Women's movement?"

I responded, "No."

He explained that it wasn't that the Women's Movement was a bad thing, it was that if they had involved the men, there may have been fewer divorces and more support from men. I brought this back to the steering committee, saying we need to involve the men somehow. We developed a strategy of "Calling out the men, Calling out the Warriors."

I went back to the Alaska Native Health Board with a new message.

"We are calling out the men, the Warriors, to stand as in the days of old, to protect their families with their lives!"

As they responded, I added, "We are asking you to end domestic violence, child sexual abuse, and child neglect in this generation."

They funded the initiative, donating $350K. Foundations also contributed and thus began the whirlwind of the work we named Family Wellness Warriors Initiative, or FWWI.

We developed one-day presentations to share our vision and gain buy-in from the church community. This began with piloting the 5-day Beauty for Ashes conference, "… to bind up the brokenhearted, to proclaim freedom for the captives and release from darkness the prisoners …. to comfort all who mourn …to bestow on them a crown of beauty instead of ashes, the oil of joy instead of mourning, and a garment of praise instead of a spirit of despair… to restore the places long devastated… for generations." Isaiah 61

We began to hold conferences. The Russian Orthodox High Priest asked to bring all his ordained Priests, students, and their wives through a Beauty for Ashes presentation. In the midst of this, I went to church with them.

While on my knees at the Russian Orthodox church, giving confession, I came to a realization. I may not have come to know the awesome holiness of God in my early youth if my mother hadn't brought us to the Russian Orthodox church. I wept for her for the first time, and with my whole heart, I forgave her all the harm she had done.

The Alaska Native people were leading the way in stopping the cycle of abuse. The call to warriors to be protectors of our children brought purpose to our efforts, and I was willing to lead the way in breaking the silence through sharing my story. I could feel my passion growing for every region in Alaska to be a place where a child could be free of harm, with no fear in their eyes. I gave my heart fully to this work God had given me to lead.

During this season of my life, I felt on top of the world, in the center of God's will.

CHAPTER 39

My own journey continued as I participated and led in BFA events, sharing my story with many. Each event brought new insight into my own life, new grief, new brokenness, new comfort and healing. I began trying to understand more deeply the longings of my heart to feel loved, affirmed, known, and deeply cared for by a man. I began to look at my journey with new understanding. I saw the pattern, repeated throughout my life, of my attempts to fill those empty places in relationships with men. It was a path of destruction, and I harmed myself and those I loved.

The longings I felt were real. They overflowed from the deepest places in my heart. I saw there had been a void in my life where I had never known fulfillment. There had been no consistent loving touch that produced the sense of being cherished by my parents. There were no words that made me feel adored and precious. Never was I held with warmth and tenderness that reached into the depths of my being, assuring me beyond a shadow of a doubt that I was loved. Domestic violence, physical and sexual abuse, doesn't provide shelter for the tenderhearted needs of children.

I had entered into adulthood, marriage, and motherhood when I was still a child myself. My longings lay dormant, like a plant gone dead for the winter. I learned to bury those longings deep inside of me early in my childhood. I didn't know they were there. I didn't realize how vulnerable these unmet needs made me.

I began to become more and more aware of the needs I had and began to look for something more. It seemed that death, tragedy, abuse, and violence were all still around us. I realized I looked to the man in my life, whoever he might be at the time, to be a source of strength, walking alongside me as life unfolded.

I had struggled with these longings and despair for much of my adult life. There were times when clouds of gloom and unhappiness would cause my emotions to spin out of control and an awakening of the buried longings would catch me by surprise. Just a tiny taste of the potential for my longings to be met felt like a jolt of electricity. It would happen when I was noticed and/or pursued by a person who seemed to know me, who would be able to really see the real me. The bottled-up emotions of the desire to be ultimately cherished, known and loved, would burst. I didn't know what to do with these feelings and I would be overwhelmed when it hit me. These longings were a wide-open door and made me feel defenseless.

I crossed that invisible line when triggered, when I felt there was no fight left in me to stay in a relationship. I became angry at my unfulfilled needs, and I directed it all at my husband. When being hurt emotionally, I took actions to protect myself. If he wasn't sensing my unspoken needs, speaking words of endearment, holding me in the night, and cherishing me in the moment, I turned away. Literally turn away.

A coldness froze my emotions. I moved into a strange place I thought would bring me a kind of freedom. In that coldness, I was freed from the cares of the world, from worrying about commitments, about those I might hurt, including myself. There, in the cold place, another's cry or tears would not impact my heart. When people attempted to warn me against the destructive path I was on, I brushed them away and turned a deaf ear toward them. I closed my eyes, my mind, and my heart to anything that may sway me. I thought I was protecting myself. Becoming hard meant placing a frozen shell about me, a fortress, a strong wall that nothing could penetrate.

Hardness

Crawl into darkness
Pull the shell up and over
It feels safe in here
But very alone.

There is no room for feelings
They are all brushed away
Only room for tasks
Drivenness without care.

Love is bottled
Tucked away and locked in
There is no sun - no rain
No senses open.

Soon awareness disappears
Pain has no hold
Just numbness and blindness
There is a strange prison-like freedom.

The shell is hardening
Soon nothing matters.
The noise is faint outside.
Eyes see through, not in.

The void now filled
No tears, sighs gone.
Come hollow laughter.
Now, I can handle life.

Hurt hurled falls flat
Touch it without emotion
It is easy to exist
All is dead inside.

In hardness
I can do anything
Go anywhere
Without worries
Without fear.

Tread down dark alleys
Run down any path

Touch the untouchables
Taste whatever I like.

I'm cold as ice
Inside the wall
Nothing harms here
I am capable of great harm.

Cannot feel
I'm without hope
There is no sunshine
And I do not care.

Even in the midst of crying out to God, I could feel my grip on making good decisions leave me. I made small choices down a destructive road that opened doors to unsafe situations and led me toward a wide path of sin. My thoughts and heart were easily turned from the man I was with, to another who would draw my attention. I believed this new person would be the "one," my answer to all my needs. I would selfishly run toward my longing, without looking toward the left or right. I would dive deep into the new relationships. I was like a pit bull once he bites into something. I had tasted the potential of my longings being met.

I wouldn't count the costs to my family. I didn't count the cost to myself. The consequences of my actions would last for years. The men in my life, our children, family and friends harmed by my choices. And I was blind to all of it.

So many times, I repented and asked God to forgive me. I would try to regain a sense of normalcy for my family. Walking out of restoration and going into deep depressions. I would walk through confessions, shame, and guilt.

I search for you and lay upon my face
I cry out for mercy
Help me, Lord, Help me!

You have given me mercy
And sweet dwelling
Healing from my sins
So many, many times

Please Lord, once more

And then came the realization. In the middle of one of the most trying events of my life, when I again had fallen into this recurring pattern, He opened my eyes to see all the harm and wrong I was doing. Deeply grieving and mourning, crying aloud, feeling the weight of all the years of failing again and again, I cried out to God, "Please do not take this cup from me until I learned everything I need to learn, so as to never return here ever again!" I wanted to know why I kept doing the same thing over and over again. Why was I going from one relationship to another?

And He answered me.

He never fails in His love for me.
He is in constant pursuit even when I push Him away.
His love is strong and His wisdom is great.
And in all this He never let me go.

While I squirm, and try to twist free,
He gently holds me to Him
Never letting me go.
With His strong, loving gaze upon me.

Even though I reached for that which harmed me
He gently held my hand to protect
He gave me allowance to learn
He drew me with His love.

Who or what can come close to this Love?
Nothing on this earth
If all my dreams and desires were granted
Yet I would not be satisfied without Him.

And then God asked me,

Where is your hope?
Who is your foundation?
Where are you looking for life?
Who or what is your anchor?

Who can awaken you and keep you alive?
What is happiness?
Who can satisfy your deepest longings?
What or who will meet your ultimate needs?

I saw what I had been doing. I saw what I had been wanting from the men in my life. I wanted them to know me, completely know me, what I was thinking and what I needed as a woman. I wanted them to fulfill all my needs. I wanted them to cherish me, love me so well that I would have no doubt of their love.

I wanted them to be God.

The Lord is my Husband
He is jealous of me
He desires to be the center of my life.
He does not want anyone or anything to take His place.

As I realized this, my eyes were opened. I asked God to forgive me for making idols out of men. There is only one true God, the Father In Heaven, the Holy Spirit, the Lord Jesus Christ. And He has promised to meet all my needs. Not any man—God. And with God, "all things are possible." I felt the chains of hell drop from me. I was freed.

God also taught me how to use Him as a refuge. After all, I was still the same person, with the same longings and needs. But God gently taught me that when longings arise, my anger flares, my needs are not met, or my tears fall, to run. He taught me to run straight under the safety of His wing, to take all my longing, my anger, my hurt, my tears straight to Him. I tuck them under His wing, and He covers me. He wraps me in His love. He holds me and meets my needs. He answers my cry.

CHAPTER 40

I have always identified with the woman at the well in the Gospel of John, chapter 4. Jesus knew her sinful past and her many husbands. Now I have hope, and my hope is in the Lord. I am not that woman. Kevin and I have been married over 20 years now, our children are grown and having children of their own. We are now great grandparents. There are obvious generational changes for the good.

Our cultural heritage is an important part of our family. My children know how to celebrate and own who they are. They know and even express in introductions of themselves that they are Caucasian, Filipino, and *Sugpiaq*.

And my children have found their voices, allowing for their own children to have a voice. They defend and watch out for one another for signs of any harm within their families. They all have their own relationships with God. They call me blessed.

Two adult children live in other states outside Alaska. They alternate every other year to come up and visit. I love watching them grow, each one on their own path. They all have life struggles, some harder than the others, but it seems like we are living as others do around us. We have more knowledge, we have some tools, we have one another, and we all have God in our lives.

For all those living in Alaska, we celebrate birthdays, weddings, Christmas Eve, and Fourth of July together. I have been at almost every one of the births of my grandchildren and some of my great-grandchildren, now numbering over 30. Each weekend children are in our home. I delight in shopping at toy stores, I know they are for the children, but I pick favorites that I delight in. Kevin and I have taken most of the families on a trip to Disneyland.

Our family loves fishing and even though Kevin really isn't an ocean voyager, he purchased a small boat that I captained and took out on fishing trips, still do this today. Halibut and salmon fishing are a dream come true. We often take trips across the bay to visit Seldovia, snagging brother Alfred to take us farther out into the bay for even better fishing excursions.

Kevin has helped me have dreams come true over and over again. Personal dreams, and family dreams of connecting with our children and always having opportunities to spend a lot of time with each of them to our hearts content.

God is our continual source of strength and peace.

He Holds Me

I cried for mercy—my face to the ground
Yet I will trust Him for He is my keeper
In the midst of madness
I will cling to the foot of the Cross.

So here I am

Pain come, I am willing
Let me step into it
That I might reach the other side.

Lord be my Rope
My Anchor, my Strength
Help me to first enter it
Then receive me, Lord
Heart be quiet
Rest
Be still

And this is the reason I have written my story. It is a story of hope, of hope in God. Greater than all my failures, greater than the unimaginable successes of Southcentral Foundation, and all the personal honor I have received, is the story of the undeniable love and faithfulness of God. Mine is the record of God's gentle but relentless pursuit of me to accomplish His purposes.

It is, as well, the story of my response to Him—at times characterized by my woundedness, at other times by my neediness and desperation, and at others by my willful defiance of Him. Yet when I was unfaithful, He remained faithful. When I turned my back, He still pursued me. My failures did not keep Him from accomplishing His purposes for my life and the work He had called me to. I see His hand in every part of my journey and understand His gracious intention has always been that I would find all the longings of my heart fully met in Him. Longings fulfilled, needs met, broken heart mended.

God knows my heart
He knows my failings
He knows all that took place
And understands
God is with me.
In the face of wrath
In the face of evil
He is my protector and has me by
His right hand.
Yet He will have the victory.
Yet His plans for my life will succeed.
Not I or anyone is in control.
God will prevail and yet love me.

EPILOGUE

In the summer of 2004, my husband I were in Washington, DC, for meetings. I was seeking funding for Southcentral Foundation (SCF) programs from various foundation leaders who had visited Alaska. Significant and exciting initiatives had been effectively impacting the wellness of Alaska Native and American Indians through our organization.

I would normally have been filled with excitement and anticipation the night before the meetings, but instead I found myself, in the middle of the night, struggling and wrestling with God.

I had survived a childhood of sexual abuse, alcoholism, domestic violence, and neglect. Now I was in the leadership role of a large organization, a wife, mother and grandmother. I was also a normal adult struggling spiritually and emotionally as I journeyed through the highs and lows of life.

And on this night I was on my face, crying softly while I prayed, asking God once again, if it was still possible that He might bless me. My crying awakened my husband, Kevin. He was not surprised to find me praying and crying in the night, as it was not the first time he had found me doing so.

The next morning I got out of bed and kneeled to pray over the day. Suddenly the phone rang. It was a foundation calling. As I listened, I tried to stifle the disappointment I felt. I thought a foundation CEO was calling to cancel their appointment after we had traveled so many miles to attend. But as I listened, the person said, "This is the MacArthur Foundation calling…"

He began explaining to me that I had won a MacArthur Fellowship, also known as the Genius Award. This prestigious honor was given annually to a select group of people recognized for having "shown extraordinary originality and dedication in their creative pursuits and a marked capacity for self-direction." It was in recognition of my leadership of Southcentral Foundation, leading the redesign of the entire primary care system, and the significant work in ending domestic violence through the Family Wellness Warriors Initiative. The award came with a grant of $500K.

I began to sob. Kevin had gone out to get us coffee and when he came in and saw me on my knees sobbing, he thought someone had died. I handed him the phone. I was the first Alaskan to ever be recognized by the Foundation.

Later, I asked Kevin if he knew why I had cried so hard at the news. He knew it wasn't because of the money or the recognition. It was because of the way God had answered the cry of my heart in the middle of the night, in such a huge way.

In that moment, I reflected on my life and the countless times and ways God has proven His faithfulness and love for me. In that moment of unimaginable blessing, I was overwhelmed with the grace of God.

Those who sow with tears will reap with songs of joy.
Those who go out weeping,
carrying seed to sow,
will return with songs of joy,
carrying sheaves with them.

— Psalm 126

ACKNOWLEDGMENTS

I WOULDN'T HAVE completed this book without the encouragement of my husband, Kevin Gottlieb, or of the work of the Family Wellness Warriors Initiative. I'm thankful for the editing assistance of Gordon Hanes and Bobbie Outten, and for the relentless guidance of the Holy Spirit.

ABOUT THE AUTHOR

KATHERINE GOTTLIEB holds BA, MBA, and honorary doctorate degrees from Alaska Pacific University and University of Alaska Anchorage, where she served as a trustee. She is a Visiting Scientist in Global Health and Social Medicine at Harvard Medical School, as well as a former board member of Cook Inlet Native Head Start, Alaska Native Heritage Center, and the National Library of Medicine Board of Regents.

Among Katherine's many honors are the Harry Hertz Leadership Award, two Malcolm Baldrige National Quality Awards, Director's Awards from the Indian Health Service, and the MacArthur Foundation Genius Award.

She served on the Joint Rulemaking Committee on Tribal and Federal Self Governance and on the leadership team of the Institute for Healthcare Improvement's 100 Million Healthier Lives Initiative.

As she has led the transformation of SCF into a world-class health organization renowned for its high-quality care, family has remained important to Katherine. She is a mother of six, grandmother of 31, and great grandmother of five.

She remains active at the national level on behalf of Alaska Native and American Indian policy issues. Her website is katherinegottlieb.com.

Made in the USA
Columbia, SC
07 December 2021